THE
FEARLESS
PATH

What a Movie Stuntman's Spiritual Awakening
Can Teach **You** About Success

THE FEARLESS PATH

What a Movie Stuntman's Spiritual Awakening Can Teach **You** About Success

CURTIS RIVERS

 FINDHORN PRESS

Published in 2017 by Findhorn Press, Scotland.
This is an abridged version of *The Seven Paths to Freedom*
published by Filament Publishing in 2013.

ISBN 978-1-84409-732-6

A CIP record for this title is available from the British Library.

Edited by Janelle Combelic
Cover design by Richard Crookes
Cover photo by Silvia Perinti
Interior design by Damian Keenan
Printed and bound in the USA

Published by
Findhorn Press
117-121 High Street,
Forres IV36 1AB,
Scotland, UK

t +44 (0)1309 690582
f +44 (0)131 777 2711
e info@findhornpress.com
www.findhornpress.com

Contents

Dedicated to the Rivers family.
You complete me.

About Curtis Rivers

Curtis Rivers is a highly popular 'transformational' speaker, much sought after for his ability to elicit profound and lasting changes in his audience. He has helped countless individuals and businesses to achieve the success they deserve.

As a motivational speaker, he motivates people to take action, and as an inspirational speaker he inspires people to change their thinking. However, it's as a transformational speaker that his effects are most dynamic, creating mindset change and action plans that last long after the event.

His widely recognized expertise in 'overcoming fear' began in his early working life, as a top Hollywood movie stuntman. His unique approach has served him well—he has broken two Guinness World Records, received a coveted award from the Screen Actors Guild, and been honoured with prestigious inclusion into the Hollywood Stuntmen's Hall of Fame. All of this without a single bone broken in his long, risk filled career.

Rivers now delivers powerful presentations and seminars, aimed at transforming the way people think.

Acknowledgements

I wish to express my heartfelt gratitude to the following people, without whom this book may have remained in the misty confines of the ether, another unrealized opportunity.

At the top of my list are my wonderful wife and children, who believed in me and supported me during the writing of this book. To my wife, for sacrificing cosy evenings by the fire so I could retire to bed early, and for tolerating my daily alarm clock, set early so I could get up and write.

For my children, who spoke about the publishing of this book as such a 'foregone conclusion' that they expelled any occasional doubts when the workload became great.

After four decades of study, having read several thousand books, it is difficult for me to thank everyone who influenced the writing of this book. I'd therefore like to thank everyone, living and deceased, whose words have touched my soul, lit a fire within me, and inspired me to take action.

I particularly give thanks to Wallace Wattles, for his immortal masterpiece, *The Science of Getting Rich*. I tip my hat to Napoleon Hill for his own masterpiece, *Think and Grow Rich*, inspired as he was by Wattles.

In turn, I thank Lloyd Conant, who has helped millions with his joint venture with Napoleon, The Nightingale-Conant Corporation. I also thank Lloyd for passing on Wattles' little green book, *The Science of Getting Rich*, to a certain Bob Proctor.

Special thanks to Bob Proctor for his own take on Wattles' *The Science of Getting Rich*, which inspired me to finally write the book I was destined to create.

Thanks to Rhonda Byrne for her film and book *The Secret*, which introduced me to other great thinkers like Dr. Michael Beckwith, Jack Canfield, John Assaraf, James Arthur Ray and Neale Donald Walsch. Each of these people has expanded my understanding of Universal Laws in his own unique way.

I give thanks to each and every one of you from the depth of my very being. Thank you.

"The journey of a thousand miles begins with one step."
— **LAO TZU** *(C. 4TH CENTURY BC)*

Open

This book was written with the sole purpose of unlocking the powerful potential stored deep within you. It contains in its pages the little known knowledge passed down through the misty corridors of time, by the select few.

Now it is *your* turn to be initiated into these compelling truths.

The fact that you are reading this page means you've attracted this information to you; whether you know that to be true or not, I assure you it is. All will become clear very soon, I promise.

The story you are about to read is just that—a story. Although a large proportion of the book is autobiographical, I'd like to make it clear that the canvas I paint my words upon is largely fictional. I have used a dramatic licence to condense many hours of real life conversation into single paragraphs, or several days of discussions into a single afternoon. Likewise, some events are told out of sequence and the names of people and places are altered in the interest of privacy.

Read it as a fictional story based on real events and awakenings, a tale written in such a way that many great truths have been carved into it. Like the mason's marks etched into solid rock, I hope this method will preserve the key messages of this book for many years to come.

The following story describes a fantastic journey of discovery, as I ascend a mystical mountain. The secret knowledge delivered on this magical trek came to me quite by chance.

At least, I didn't consciously set off on that fateful day in October looking for some spiritually life changing experience. Yet a life altering, paradigm shifting experience is exactly what I got.

By sharing my adventure with you, and by passing on the amazing things I discovered, I know that you too will be able to transform your life. The reality is, when you reached for this book a moment ago, you already began that journey.

On that autumn day, I was overseas to trek up a mountain that I had always dreamed of ascending, ever since I had read about it in a dusty bookshop as a small child. I'm not speaking of Everest, nor of K2 or the Matterhorn, but a mystical mountain off the usual tourist trail.

As well as writing this book in story form to convey important wisdom to you, I've also written it in layers, and dropped in the odd clue here and there, just for fun.

There are clues hidden on many degrees in my multi-layered book.

Some will speak fully to your conscious mind; others will creep into your subconscious region. Some messages will not enter your mind until you're reading this book for the second time, or third—to be frank, it's been written in that way just for you!

Sometimes you might enjoy other parts of this book without realizing all along that perplexing codes were aptly encoding some amazing knowledge within!

Sound a bit farfetched? Not possible? I will promise you that it is. Better still, I will now go straight ahead to prove it to you. Let's look carefully over this page for example. Quite ordinary, wouldn't you say? Worry not – it gets better! So, are you still not aware that right here and now, this minute, you are reading hidden code? Well you are! So go ahead and count the twenty-five letters to witness the code, from the words "There are clues hidden..." above. A short message will slowly appear before your eyes. Go ahead and read it! Start by carefully counting the letter 'T' as 'one', then you draw around every twenty-fifth hidden letter in the sentence. You'll get 'y' first, and 'o' next, so circle these and count another twenty-five letters to circle the next one – and so on and so forth.

Did you get the message? Or did you decide to skip that bit and come back to it later? I thought so. That's why I dropped it in there, just to see if you were a 'doer' or a 'when I get around to it' type of person!

Did you consider doing the exercise, but had no pen or pencil close by? Again, not really a valid excuse, as I'm sure you could find one if you really wanted to!

OK, you don't have to do the exercise if you don't want to, but having a pencil and paper close by is going to become extremely useful as you read this book over the next seven days.

If you did the counting and the circling of letters, you'll believe me now about the multi-layered, hidden and hypnotic writing within this book. You'll be starting to realize that this book might just be the one you've been looking for. Sit back, relax, and enjoy the journey.

Still regretting not having a pencil handy? OK, for those without pencils, the hidden message was a quote by the late, great, Sir Winston Churchill, who uncovered some of the truths shared in this book during his own travels and studies. I'll highlight every twenty-fifth letter here for you:

There are clues hidden on many degrees in my multi-layered book. Some will speak fully to your conscious mind; others will creep into your subconscious region. Some messages will not enter your mind until you're reading this book for the second time, or third – to be frank, it's been written in that way just for you!

Sometimes you might enjoy other parts of this book without realising all along that perplexing codes were aptly encoding some amazing knowledge within.

Sound a bit farfetched? Not possible? I will promise you that it is. Better still, I will now go straight ahead to prove it to you. Let's look carefully over this page for example. Quite ordinary, wouldn't you say? Worry not – it gets better! So are you still not aware that right here and now, this minute, you are reading hidden code? Well – you are! So go ahead and count the twenty-five letters to witness the code, from the words "There are clues hidden…" above. A short message will slowly appear before your eyes! Go ahead and read it! Start by carefully counting the letter 'T' as 'one', then you draw around every twenty-fifth hidden letter in the sentence. You'll get 'y' first, and 'o' next, so circle these and count another twenty-five letters to circle the next one – and so on and so forth.

"You create your own universe as you go along."

Sir Winston Churchill knew a great secret! Many of history's most eminent high-achieving heroes knew the same coveted fact. It's just one of a number of truths that I'm going to happily share with you over the next seven days or so—hidden gems that are exceptionally powerful and life altering. Trust me; you're going to cherish this book!

Why seven days? Well, after arriving at the foot of this sacred mountain, my own journey took just seven days.

From setting off to reaching the summit, seven days. Each day ended at a very special place, and it is the sacred and magical knowledge that was shared with me during this amazing trek that I wish to share with you.

I recommend that you read just one chapter a day—seven chapters, seven days—so you can soak up and process the information in the same way that I did in the story you're about to read.

Beyond that, there will be exercises you'll want to return to as the information settles in. It is my sincere hope that you will come back to this book often, as you slowly begin to see your life change beyond all recognition.

Mine has. All I did was apply these simple lessons. Once I share my story, you will be able to apply those same lessons to your own life, and follow in the footsteps of some of the greatest people ever to walk this fabulous planet.

Let us begin, then, early one sunny morning, by a low, crumbling wall at the edge of a remote village, as I await the arrival of my mountain guide.

CHAPTER ONE

*"To believe in the things you can see and
can touch is no belief at all;
but to believe in the unseen
is both a triumph and a blessing."*
— ABRAHAM LINCOLN *(1809–1865)*

Believe

I put my weight on the crumbling wall and almost fell right through. A quick scramble to my feet and a cursory glance around to establish my stumble had gone unseen, and I returned my gaze to the end of the track where I expected my guide to appear.

He was late, which wasn't a great start, and I felt really ill, which was worse. That's why I'd tried to rest against the wall—I had a banging headache, a chesty cough, and a streaming nose.

How could this be happening? I kept myself really fit; it was part of my job.

I had earned my living up until this point as a television and movie stuntman, or 'stunt performer'. Even in those quiet times between bookings, I had to maintain a good level of physical strength and agility. One way I did this was by walking and trekking.

Bored senseless by the routine plodding on the gym's jogging machines and the monotonous climbing on cross trainers, I swapped the view of plasma screens for the open vistas of the countryside and never looked back.

I walk four or five miles a day now, every day when it's at all possible, early in the morning before showering. I burn more calories on my one-hour daily walk than I ever did on those machines, and I use the time to reflect and plan the day ahead.

This explains how I came to be in this mystical place by the crumbling wall, but doesn't yet explain why I was alone.

Going It Alone

I wished my wife were with me to see this. I often thought about her; she'd missed so many spectacular experiences. But she simply didn't want to go.

Her love for adventure had been challenged just before the kids came along, when one of my backpack adventures across Egypt backfired. She had food poisoning, sunburn, and far too much attention from the locals who kept grabbing her long blonde hair. The arduous night train to Cairo was the final straw. Even riding camels to the Great Pyramids at sunrise proved too little, too late. She wanted to hide for the remainder of the trip, which she did in a cosy little hotel on an island in the river Nile, just upstream from the wonderful city of Luxor. I cycled from our base to visit nearby temples and to practise my Egyptian (I learned to speak Egyptian Arabic before my first trip to Egypt) while she lay by the pool. I loved it. Unfortunately, she didn't.

In order to satisfy my own desire to see the world I had to rely on the occasional overseas stunt job. *The Count of Monte Cristo*, for example, took me to Ireland, Malta and Comino. I doubled for the Count, played by Jim Caviezel, performing some riding and underwater sequences. I also returned to Malta a few years later to work with Sir David Jason on *Ghostboat*. There were other opportunities, like a commercial filmed in Turkey and a Viking movie in Iceland, but the international trips were few and far between.

Family vacations we mainly took in England while the children were young. Although I loved these holidays, I found it more and more difficult to hide my growing frustrations from my wife. I had such a burning desire to see all of the wonders that the world had to offer! After tolerating my moaning for some time, she eventually relented.

I had her blessing to travel alone. Fantastic!

So it was that I took my family to the sunny English coastlines of Cornwall and Devon, or perhaps to the French Riviera once a year, but I also left a couple of weeks free every year to have an adventure of my own.

"Mr Rivers!"

An antique Jeep ground to a halt in front of me, belching plumes of acrid fumes from its rear end.

This can't be the guide, I thought of the large, rotund man, sweating profusely behind the wheel.

"I'm sorry for the delay," he said, and explained that the guide intended for my trip had gone astray, but he'd been lucky enough to source another guide locally.

I wasn't impressed at all.

My headache was getting worse, not helped by the stress of having to wait so long, only to find someone, somewhere, had screwed up. I accepted the big guy's apology and asked where this 'local' guide was. The driver pointed to a field a short distance away, where someone stood motionless against a backdrop of lush green mountains, framed by a deep blue sky.

A Chance Encounter

I squeezed through a gap in the wall and began to ascend the steep dirt track that led to my new travelling partner, who was making adjustments to his load.

As I approached, I was surprised to find that this small man, about five feet six inches tall, was not local at all; he looked European, and I became slightly apprehensive on realizing he was a lot older than me.

I needn't have worried. As I got within twenty feet of this man, his face lit up like a child walking into a room full of Christmas presents. His white, wispy beard contrasted starkly with his leathery, sunned skin.

"Welcome," he said, in the gentlest voice I had ever heard. His English was excellent, and his tone reminded me of Albus Dumbledore in the first *Harry Potter* movies, played by the late, great Richard Harris. (I was fortunate enough to appear in a *Harry Potter* film myself; I played a Death Eater in *Harry Potter and the Order of the Phoenix*. Unfortunately, by that time Richard Harris had shed his mortal coil, to be replaced, rather well I think, by Michael Gambon.)

I knew right away that I was in the presence of an Englishman who had fallen in love with this place during an expedition, many years previously. I suddenly felt at ease, with a nervous excitement for what adventure might unfold over the coming days.

"I have been looking forward to this very much," he continued, which I found odd because he'd only just been chosen to lead me up the mountain, according to the chap in the Jeep. He spoke in whispers that made me hang on to his every word, punctuating his sentences with loud, passionate phrases, always followed by a broad smile.

He looked so intensely into my eyes when he spoke that I felt he was looking into my soul and me into his. There was an air of timelessness in his gaze that is difficult to explain, except to say that for a guy who was probably in his sixties, his eyes seemed to be one hundred years old.

His dark green jacket seemed oddly out of place, more suited to an English country pheasant shoot than a mountain ascent. This chap was 'old school' in the extreme: sturdy boots with a couple of pairs of long woollen socks, the outer turned over the boot, the inner pulled up to just below the knee, where a thick pair of old olive trousers were tucked. The jacket almost covered a light brown woollen scarf that was too long and protruded from the bottom of the coat.

"Come," he said. "Let us begin this journey."

The Journey Begins

His pace was slow and deliberate up the first grassy foothill. A well-trodden path eased me into the walk. The relatively flat ground began to slowly increase in steepness, while the path began to twist up the hill like a python hunting its prey.

It must have been the nerves that kept me talking incessantly for that first hour of our trek. I was essentially a very shy and private person—the kind of person to feel awkward at parties, the sort you'd find pretending to be interested in the CDs or hanging out by the buffet table.

My burning legs breathed a sigh of relief as we reached the top of the first high foothill and began a steady descent into the lush valley below. A beautiful lake at the bottom of the slope caused me to wonder if this new guide was taking me on a different route to the one I'd arranged with the travel company. There was certainly no mention of a lake in my detailed itinerary.

The guide hadn't said much at all to me so far, which is probably why I was sweating and out of breath, while he looked as fresh as the mountain air that whispered up from the lake and cooled my moist brow.

"I'm sorry," I said. "I was feeling quite unwell when we met and I didn't get your name?"

"Pierce," said the guide without turning around, "but the locals call me Harry. I prefer Pierce."

"As in Brosnan?" I replied, a little surprised.

The guide stopped, and turned around with a frown.

"Indeed, I suppose exactly as in Brosnan."

He paused, and inhaled as if he was going to add something, but instead placed an index finger against his lips, turned, and continued his descent towards the lake, which was now drawing near.

I considered telling him that I'd had a few scenes with Pierce Brosnan in the Bond movie *Tomorrow Never Dies*, or telling him how

I'd been asked to double Pierce in an underwater scene in the same movie, but somehow, I figured he'd be largely unimpressed. There was something about him that made me feel he'd been to a lot of places and achieved an awful lot.

Much to my surprise, on our arrival at the lake, he made his way to a small boat tied up at a tiny makeshift jetty.

I was confused as to why we were getting into a boat, but before I could ask him he'd taken up the oars, pushed off, and sped from the shore like a Cambridge Blue!

"Oh," I said. "Listen, I'm happy to row. It's just a cold I've picked up."

"Thank you," he replied, as I began to cough and hold my chest. "But do you know which way we are going?"

"Er, no."

"Good," he said with a warm smile. "Then it is settled."

With that, he picked up the pace, seeming to delight in the strength and fitness he was demonstrating from a man much older than I.

Ahead of us the towering mountain grew taller and taller as we crossed the lake.

"Wow!" I remarked. "It looks a heck of a lot bigger in real life."

The patient guide smiled, as he eased off the rowing, lifting the oars out of the cold water.

"Yes, indeed," he said, looking down at his boots. With his head held low, his deep eyes flicked up to engage mine. "If you think that little foothill is high, wait until you see the actual mountain beyond it!"

He silently placed the oars back into the water, and pulled hard to continue our crossing. I sighted a long thin boat to our starboard side (that's the right hand side for those of you who prefer to stay on dry land).

It was the first time I'd seen a boat like that—wide enough for four people to sit side by side, yet long enough to fit dozens of people if required. Like a Viking longboat, its bow and stern lifted from the lake and curved upwards, yet in place of the mast and sails, a small tented canopy was held aloft by four wooden poles. It looked like a garden gazebo stuck in the middle of a small longboat.

Pierce explained that it was a local fishing boat, and indeed as we drew closer I could see the nets being dragged in by children. One of the nets got snagged on an oar. The children didn't seem fazed by this; in fact they seemed to find it quite amusing. Some adults scolded the children as their catch began to slip back into the waters, and ran from the stern to help. The boat rocked from side to side, suddenly looking quite unstable. Pierce stopped rowing and pointed as the boat groaned and a couple of children fell from the side and into the cold lake. Then it lurched back and capsized completely!

My heart raced as I began to unzip my jacket, instinct preparing me to dive straight in and save anyone I could. However, before I could get my arm out of my jacket, Pierce let out an enormous belly laugh.

Both the children and the adults were smiling and laughing as they splashed around, some clutching floating bags, others treading water, and some holding on tight to the upturned boat.

"They will be fine," Pierce said, wiping a laughter tear from his eye. "Their rescuers are already on their way."

He gestured to the bank, where a similar boat was now racing in their direction, its oars beating in perfect unison.

"You know," he whispered, with a distant look in his eye, "I find that this wonderful gift of life can be likened to such a shipwreck."

"Yes," I replied, a little uncomfortably, "I know what you mean."

I had no idea what he meant.

A Life on the Ocean Waves

I just assumed he was going to tell me of his failed marriage, or how his children or grandchildren never visit anymore. I was wrong, again. What he shared with me on that boat made me think deeply for the first time in quite a while.

"You see," he continued, "we are born into this life, like the survivors of a sunken ship who wake the next morning, adrift on the ocean with their fellow passengers. Carried like corks upon the water, we drift with the ebb and flow of the tides, at the mercy of where nature takes us. Like everyone else, we accept our lot, and hope beyond hope that we will reach dry land before it is too late.

"Most people do not realize that all they have to do is swim away from the others, swim away from that crowd that floats adrift on the ocean of life.

"Save yourself," he said as we neared shore. "Swim away with your sights fixed firmly on paradise, and you will soon feel that warm, dry sand between your toes."

I nodded politely as he helped me onto the wet pebbled beach, trying not to show that his comments had stirred something deep within me.

Making our way upwards through deep grass and sweet smelling vegetation, I pondered on what he had said on the lake. I used to be one of those people who had swum away from the crowd. In my late teens, I could set my sights on anything in the world, no matter how preposterous, and achieve that goal. I learned to fly, I learned to ride a horse, I got that black belt and taught those fencing classes. In my twenties, I visited those places I'd longed to see, like Niagara Falls and the Grand Canyon. I became that movie stuntman I'd always wanted to be.

In my early thirties, I managed to break a couple of Guinness World Records. So why, as I approached the latter part of my thirties, did I find myself adrift on the sea of life with everyone else?

How had I come to 'accept' my lot in life, and just 'make do' with what I had? I wasn't happy in my work, I didn't like the majority of the back-stabbing people I worked with in the television and film industries. Many of my relationships with friends and relatives had crumbled to dust. My house was a bitter disappointment—still stuck in a three-bedroom semi-detached house in a small ex-mining town near Nottingham. My car was old and boring. Life was becoming a stale ritual of balancing finances in order to survive from one month to the next, perhaps squirrelling enough away to go on the occasional holiday.

Where had it all gone wrong? "We should rest now," Pierce said, removing the large blanket-wrapped bundle from his back. "Let us eat a moment, and chat about your loss of direction."

"I Can Teach You Much"

You could have knocked me over with a feather! Was I that easy to read?

The guy had climbed ahead since we crossed the lake, and I rarely saw him look back. So how could he know what I was thinking? I guessed he said similar things to other tourist climbers, and had a similar pensive response from his listeners.

"I am gifted with a great open mind," he said, slicing the skin of a mango with his sharp knife. "I can teach you much, remind you of what you already know to be true deep down, but you must keep an open mind as I explain. Can you do this? Are you prepared to believe?" he said, eating the mango flesh.

"Yes, of course," I coughed, happy to just sit back and give my aching back and legs a rest and to catch my breath. I had found it increasingly difficult to breathe for the last hour of ascent.

He wiped his mouth. "You see, if your mind is not open, you will replace positive acceptance with negative doubt. You attract into your life *exactly* what you hold in your mind for a sustained period."

He unscrewed the cap of an antique water bottle and took a sip.

"*You attract into your life exactly what you hold in your mind for a sustained period of time.* This is the basic principle in life that so many overlook.

"Thoughts of doubt attract more doubt into your life. By thinking doubt with your mind, you *feel* doubt in your heart.

"Thoughts of worry attract more worry into your life. By worrying in your mind, you *feel* that heavy feeling of worry in your heart. When you feel worry, you attract more things, people and circumstances into your life that cause you to worry.

"This is *the* great law of life, as real as the law of gravity, and quite obvious when you sit and think about it.

"The reverse is also true: thoughts of love, *feeling* love, can only attract more people, circumstances and opportunities that lead you to experience more love in your life.

"If I could teach you how to hold a worthy thought in your mind, then you must believe me when I tell you that you will observe that very thing in the real world. It will cease to exist in the world of thought, and come to exist in the world of form.

"All you have to do is learn to keep that positive image there, in spite of conflicting images in your temporary surrounds.

"You must *believe* in that image and it will very soon become your waking reality."

He went on to explain how everything we see in the physical world only exists because it was first thought of in the mind. For example, to create a new book cover, the designer must think the thought first, before choosing the photo he or she will use, or typing out the title on their computer. It's obvious when you think about it: everything in this world, from cola cans to lamp posts, road signs to package designs, cars to planes, pencils to printers, everything must have appeared in the mind before its creation.

Pierce's words got me thinking about some of the things that I'd achieved in my life. I'd thought of nothing but becoming a stuntman for years.

No matter what the setback or injury I sustained in my training, it never stopped me thinking about how great it was going to be when I became a movie stuntman. I thought about it all the time, I collected newspaper cuttings on stuntmen, I recorded TV shows about stuntmen. When eBay was launched I even collected memorabilia about stuntmen! After holding that thought in my mind, unwavering, I became a stuntman.

Many others had considered a career as a stuntman, then allowed their attention to drift and consider other careers. That image in their mind of becoming a stuntman became fuzzy as they considered other options. They never became stuntmen.

I've met many of those people in my life, who smile and say "Wow. I wanted to be a stuntman when I left school" or "I started training to become a stuntman when I left the army." Others actually began their gruelling training to become a movie stuntman, and spent many thousands in the process. However, somewhere during that training, they stopped visualizing being a stuntman. Maybe they'd had an injury learning a martial art, or failed a diving test, or fell from a horse when learning to show jump. Whatever the reason, they began to doubt. Perhaps they thought, "Maybe this isn't for me" or "I'm not cut out for this" and replaced that image of success in their mind with one of defeat. None of those people became stuntmen.

I considered my own mindset again, this time with regard to breaking records. I'd thought of breaking a parachuting World Record since the age of 18. In my mind, I'd taken off in that hot air balloon wearing an oxygen mask hundreds of times. I thought about it all of the time with passion and enthusiasm. I collected newspaper cuttings on parachuting and hot air balloon adventures, I recorded TV shows about the subject, and used eBay to collect hot air balloon and parachute record memorabilia. In 2002, having held that thought in my mind for years, I broke two World Records—both using a hot air balloon, and both involving parachuting from high above the earth.

Perhaps, I thought, Pierce is onto something here.

"What I tell you is true," he continued, putting on his backpack. "If I can succeed in teaching you how to really think about what you desire, then you will succeed in manifesting those desires in your life. It is as simple as that.

"Tell me, if what I am telling you were true, and there were absolutely no limits to what you could experience, or where you could experience it—if you could mix with the sort of people you really wanted to mix with, live in the house you always dreamed of, drive the car you always wanted to drive—what would you desire? What do you want? What do you *really* want? The transformation of your life begins with this simple step: decide what you want, and write it down."

I clicked shut the straps of my rucksack beside me on the ground and nodded.

"I'm serious," he said. "Write them down."

"What, now?" I said in disbelief. It was late afternoon and we'd covered a lot of ground. My back and legs were aching, my head still pounded, my cough seemed to be getting worse, and now I had blisters. The last thing I wanted to do was stop and play games. I just wanted to finish today's walk, the longest trek planned in the week ahead, and get my head down for some much needed rest.

"You *could* do it now," he replied. "It depends on you. If you *really* want to transform your life." He turned around, and smiled knowingly. "Let us complete today's walk. Perhaps you should rest a while as you consider these things. We have time. Do not worry about that. Not far to the temple now. You can draw up your list there, before supper."

"The temple?" I enquired, turning to pick up my rucksack and digging deep for the strength to climb further. "What temple? I thought we'd be…"

As I turned around to throw my backpack into place, he was gone.

"This way, my friend. Not far now!" His voice was carried on a cool breeze from somewhere in front of me.

As I glanced up, his head reappeared above a grassy mound some 50 feet ahead, his broad smile mocking my inexperience on the mountain. Before I could say another word, he was gone, leaving me with no choice but to grit my teeth and walk fast.

When I caught him up, he nodded like a father impressed by a child's stamina, kept his head low, and plodded on in silence. His words echoed around my head like the desperate cries of a fallen climber inside a deep crevasse. *"What do you want? If you could have, be, or do anything, what would it be?"*

Like a lot of people, I considered winning the lottery as a good starting point. However, I knew Pierce would dig deeper. Why the lottery? Did I want to be a multimillionaire? Was it the pile of cash that I wanted, or the life that kind of money could buy? If it were the life, then what did that life look like—what did I *really* want?

By the time we arrived at the small village some 4,000 feet above where we had begun our journey, my mind and body had been stretched to their limits. My headache was only just starting to ease off, my cough and runny nose made me feel sorry for myself, my aching legs and back did nothing to uplift me, and my blistered right foot burned as if I were standing on red hot sand.

Making our way past the shoddy buildings, Pierce pointed to a strange run-down temple at the end of the street. It was a muddy red colour, possibly wood, with mud and dung thrown against the walls to strengthen it. Not at all what I was expecting. I was also surprised by the 'vibe' I got from the villagers.

Instead of welcoming smiles, I received wary looks. Before I could ask, Pierce whispered, "The people here can be quite nasty to each other. Jealousy is rife, and despair fills their souls. They are racked with guilt and fear and have forgotten the old ways, which does not serve them well. We will be more welcome in the temple. Come, I have arranged a room for the night with my friends."

Villagers began to stop and stare as Pierce knocked on the door with his bare fist, sending a distant echo around the temple like a boulder smashing its way down a canyon. The crowd gathered and began to murmur. I found myself relieved when the large wooden door began to open inwards, to reveal a bald-headed temple worker.

Enter the Temple

"Welcome," whispered the gatekeeper, looking straight at me. "You come to rest for one night?"

I looked to Pierce, who stood smiling at me, but he said nothing.

"Er, yes please. Just the one night."

"Very well. You are most welcome," replied the temple worker. He gestured for us to come inside.

The gathering crowd fell back with the closing of the huge doors, and the dropping of the wooden beam secured the place. Despite the very basic surrounds, this felt like sanctuary.

The temple worker bowed and led me between small buildings adorned with long red flags. I struggled for breath at first, as the air was filled with such a strong aroma of incense. The door to my room revealed a basic layout: a bed on the floor, with plenty of light from a window with shutters. Nothing else.

The sight of the bed alone was a most welcome one after a long day's walking. The toilet and wash facilities were close by, and this was far better than climbing into a sleeping bag inside a tent, which I'd been expecting.

"You rest a while? Then eat?" asked the temple worker.

"Yes please," I replied. "If that's OK?"

"Of course. You rest, I come back later so you can eat with us."

With that, he bowed and backed out of the room, quietly closing the door behind him. That's when it hit me. This place was *so* quiet. I wondered if it was because it was a small temple, and only held a few people. Maybe the occupants were praying or meditating.

I flopped onto the bed fully clothed and stretched out in sheer bliss. In the silence of this sacred place, I realized that my headache had finally gone. Despite the remaining breathlessness, cough, runny nose, aches and pains in my back and legs, and blisters on my toes, I actually felt happy, at ease with the world and with myself.

As the tide of tiredness crept ashore, I reflected once more upon the day's events.

The last minute change of guide, the morning's walking, the trip across the lake, the remainder of the day's trekking. And all the while, the guide's gentle advice. That slow, soothing whisper.

"If I could teach you how to hold a worthy thought in your mind, then you must believe me when I tell you that you will observe that very thing in the real world. It will cease to exist in the world of thought, and come to exist in the world of form."

I'd already pondered on how that related to me becoming a professional movie stunt performer against all of the odds. And then breaking those World Records for high altitude parachuting.

It felt like a jigsaw piece had been dropped into place by Pierce but my mind was resisting it slightly, not quite letting it click. I wanted this to be true, but if it was, then the knowledge could change everything. It *would* change everything.

As my body relaxed into the straw mattress, and my breathing became deep, I remembered the first expedition I organized at the age of 22.

Here was another example of me coming up with something I really wanted to do, and making it happen, despite everyone around me telling me it could not be done.

| The Romanian Expedition |

It wasn't long after the Romanian Revolution, and poverty was rife. Children were dying there every day due to the lack of simple medicines we took for granted in the West. What I proposed was to remove the back seats from my Citroen Visa, fill the car with life-saving pills, and drive overland from England to Romania, where I would stop when I reached the Black Sea. I'd locate the hospital in Constanţa I'd been in touch with, and deliver the medicines.

I was 22, and I had never left the UK.

I had never been overseas as a kid. We took our summer vacations in England, usually not too far from where we lived. Neither of my parents could drive, so we could only go as far as the bus or train could take us. Flying overseas was never even considered; that was the sort of thing 'rich people' did. So we'd have a day out here and a day out there, sometimes to Redcar, the beach five miles from where we lived, and occasionally Saltburn, on the same stretch of North Sea coastline, some ten miles away.

I wouldn't change those holidays for the world. It never occurred to me that we were poor, or not travelling far; I was with the people that I loved. Digging a sandcastle in Redcar felt like surfing in Hawaii to me.

My expedition to Romania was greeted with scepticism by my family. Friends and family told me I wouldn't make it.

I thought of little besides the Romanian expedition for months. I used to become obsessed with my goals. I worked in a school at the time as a technician and spent my spare time typing letters and sending faxes around the UK and to places like the Municipal Hospital in Constanţa. I made calls to aid groups for advice on the journey, to government officials, and to local politicians. My bedroom became the nerve centre of the operation, a large map of Europe on my bedroom wall with map pins indicating key points on the route, like border crossings and danger zones, and surrounded by dozens of Post-it notes.

I had no money, but I'd unwittingly tapped into the great Universal Law that Pierce was telling me about. I held the image in my mind of arriving in Constanţa with the medical supplies. I imagined not only what it would look like when we reached the Black Sea after such an epic journey across the whole of Europe, but what it would *feel* like.

The sun on my face, the wind in my hair, the smell of the sea, the sound of the gulls—I was excited by it, as if it was 100% guaranteed. In my mind I travelled daily through France, Belgium, Holland, Germany, Austria, Hungary, and Romania.

By the time I was due to leave for Romania, everything had dropped into place. All of the medicines were donated; a local Citroen garage serviced my car free of charge; the Mayor gave me a special letter; my employer paid my wages while I was away; and there were many other donations.

I did indeed feel blessed.

Outward Bound

I was travelling with Sven, an older guy I'd met at a local Family History Centre ran by The Church of Jesus Christ of Latter-day Saints. A former manic depressive, still on medication, he seemed to have had a string of bad luck in his life. I thought it might expand his mind, and cheer him up a little. The only downside was that he didn't drive. Not only that, but it quickly became evident that Sven simply couldn't understand road maps, compass bearings, or road signs. He was to be a passenger taking the grand tour, and I was to be his chauffeur. During the trip, I was sometimes frustrated at having to do every single task, but most grumblings evaporated at the satisfaction of seeing Sven smile like I'd never seen before.

By repeatedly visualizing the different points of the journey ahead of time, I had unknowingly made it easy for me to navigate through the various countries in record time. Within just a few days, we'd already enjoyed the diverse cultures of five different countries, from the flat lands of western France and Holland to the snow-capped mountains of Austria.

Along the way, we'd 'bump into someone' and start chatting. They would become friendly and give great advice, and then tell us of someone they knew further along the route who might be able to help. That person would then pass on contact details of a friend in the next country who might also be able to help. It was wonderful to be carried along like that, with everything falling perfectly into place.

For instance, Michoül (pronounced Mick-ale) lived with his wife Anita in Vienna. He'd recently made the trip to Romania with a small convoy of cars and was glad to get out of the experience in one piece. Michoül mentioned the gangs of bandits that preyed on Westerners in the Romanian mountain routes we'd be passing through, and told horror stories about the border crossings into Hungary and Romania. He suggested we pose as Red Cross officials and also carry Coca-Cola and Cadbury's chocolate bars to bribe border officials.

We left Vienna around 5.30 p.m. and travelled towards the Hungarian border, arriving shortly after dark. As we approached, we began to see a lot of trucks pulled up along the roadside. We must have been two miles from the border when we started to really slow down and take stock of what we'd let ourselves in for.

In the end, after being shunted from guard to guard and sweating through some scary moments, we sailed through in less than two hours. All thanks to the Mayor's letter, a load of Coca-Cola and Cadbury bars, and smiling confidence on my part. I breathed a sigh of relief on Hungarian soil.

| The Hospitality of Strangers |

I drove non-stop after crossing the border, then we slept in the car somewhere on the outskirts of Budapest.

Finances were low and we didn't have any local currency (forints) as we'd only just arrived and planned to keep driving through the whole country if we could. At 6 a.m., strolling through the grounds of a nearby church to stretch my legs and get some fresh air, with my stomach rumbling, pockets empty, the furthest from home I'd ever been, in a country where I didn't speak the language, life seemed a little bleak.

Just then, a middle-aged lady walking through the otherwise deserted park paused, turned, and nervously said something in Hungarian to me. When I smiled and said, "Sorry, I..." she interjected with a broader smile, "English?"

It turned out she was a private English tutor!

Better still, once I told our story, there was an instant connection between us. She saw we were good people who were genuinely trying to help for the pleasure of giving.

Before I knew it, I was enjoying her company over a plate of Hungarian beef and pommes frites and she insisted on paying for everything. She looked upon it as a rare chance to converse with real English people, to test her language skills and ask lots of questions to help in her tutoring, while doing her good deed.

She was a lovely lady who not only filled my belly, but warmed my heart. It's always great to be reminded that the world is full of good, honest and giving people.

After leaving Budapest we headed to the Eastern border of Hungary, and arrived under a large full moon. This time, the border crossing was relatively effortless. One box of chocolates and two litres of Coca-Cola later, we drove into the moonlit blackness of Romania. We had reached the country of our final destination, and it felt superb.

With no street lighting, no cat's eyes, no illuminated or reflective signs, we had only our headlights and the moon to navigate the dusty Romanian road, where the potholes were six feet across and one foot deep. The edge of the road had often fallen away into the field next to it, and we had to be prepared to stop quickly for horse-drawn carts at two in the morning or for a stationary lorry with its lights off. I soldiered on through the night, arriving at Cluj-Napoca at 4.30 a.m.

Our next hosts were Doctor Michai (Dodo to his friends) and his wife Gabbi in Cluj-Napoca, who overwhelmed us with their generosity. We were strangers, yet they gave so much, and asked for nothing in return. They even set us up with our next contact, Valeriu Petresco, who was to put us up for the night in Bucharest.

Between the two safe houses of Dodo in Cluj and Valeriu in Bucharest stood 275 miles of makeshift road over the Transylvanian Alps. In my old Citroen Visa, it took seven arduous hours of challenging and relentless driving, but we did it.

Like all of the people who helped us on our way to the hospital in Constanţa, Valeriu was exceptionally kind and giving. After putting us up for the night in his comfortable Bucharest home, and following a satisfying breakfast, we were ready for the final leg of our trip—a three-hour drive east to the Black Sea coast and the town of Constanţa.

| The Beauty of the Black Sea |

The final leg of the outward journey was truly breathtaking. It was like going back in time, as the roads turned into tracks, roof tiles to thatch, and the houses to small dwellings. At a crossroads where I stopped to check my map I noticed a man ploughing a field using a plough that looked 1,000 years old, made from roughly shaped branches and what looked like a thin stone as the shoe that turned the earth.

Every time I took a wrong turn and headed off the beaten track the locals would look at us in wonder as if they'd not seen a car before. To be honest, they probably hadn't seen many at all when I think of some of the dead end tracks I tried to negotiate in some of those villages!

The roads began to improve slightly (some of the bomb craters filled with earth) and the rural villages gave way to more urban surrounds. Then I caught sight of the Black Sea! I felt both achievement and relief, like a marathon runner approaching the final half mile and sensing the winning line.

What really surprised me was that the sea really was black! I'd seen the Red Sea in photos, and it looked as blue as any other sea, so I expected the Black Sea to be the same. Perhaps it was the seabed, or the depth of the water at that point, or the light at that time of the day. Whatever the reason, it was a perfect way to see our destination for the first time.

When we arrived at the hospital, our donation was greeted with tears of gratitude from the doctors and nurses, who wasted no time in distributing the pills to different rooms and administering them to the children right away. It felt like arriving at a drought-stricken school with bottles of fresh drinking water.

I suppressed the feeling that I could have brought more. Short of learning to drive a truck or organizing a convoy, I'd done my very best. I was just one of many people doing their bit to help a country in crisis at that time, and collectively we were making a positive difference to lots of lives. It felt fantastic.

When the initial frenzy of unloading the supplies had subsided, we were given a tour of the facility and introduced to the staff. Spending time with the children was highly emotional. We played with the children, hugged them, and stroked their hair if they were too ill to get out of bed. The odd child would not make it until the next day, others would now face a brighter future with the drugs we'd brought along.

We stayed at a hotel for the first time that night, a treat to reward ourselves for successfully getting the supplies to the hospital. After the best sleep in several weeks, we rose early and returned to the hospital.

I hadn't expected to want to stay at this place, yet I did. I really wanted to stay on and help out in some way. The truth was, however, my skills were better used elsewhere; I had little to offer the hospital but my love and understanding. The drugs had been safely delivered the previous day, and it was now time to step aside, let the doctors and nurses do their work.

After a tearful farewell, we decided to take a closer look at the Black Sea before starting the long journey home.

From the beach the sea looked blue now and, lit by the soothing sunshine, she drew me in like a temptress. At the water's edge, she breathed a gentle, warming breeze that teased my hair, and begged for me to stay a while longer. I closed my eyes, breathed in the moment, and then turned my back and walked away. It was time to go home.

| Homeward Bound |

The goal of the trip had been the safe delivery of the drugs to the hospital on the Black Sea, to help save the children. I had visualized every aspect of getting there, not coming back! My thinking was, "If we can drive all the way to the Black Sea from England, I'm sure we can get back OK."

The return leg then, was a different matter, fraught with every kind of challenge imaginable. We were lost within minutes of leaving the beach, and the man I asked for directions led us to a dead-end where a gang of his friends tried to rob us. We barely escaped with our lives.

Another problem was Sven. His mental health had started to deteriorate before we got to Romania. He'd stopped talking, washing, shaving and brushing his teeth. It turned out that he'd decided he no longer needed his anti-depressant medication back in Austria. Travel, he deduced, was all he needed, not medication that dulled his senses. By Romania he was becoming clinically depressed again, argumentative and a little paranoid. I did my best to be patient with him but it started to wear me down.

In Bulgaria we hugged the Black Sea coast until dark, but when I pulled onto a beach the car got stuck in the sand; police dragged us out the next morning. Then we were refused entry into Turkey by trigger-happy border guards.

Diverting inland to Sofia, Sven finally agreed to help; what he did was fill the car with diesel but my car ran on unleaded petrol and we had to get a mechanic to drain it.

Then we kept getting lost as roads turned to dirt tracks and flat plains to mountains; after a day of stomach-churning driving on snaking roads on the edge of high cliffs, we finally arrived at the border crossing, but it was the wrong country—rather than Greece we faced war-torn Yugoslavia.

Forced to turn around, I had to do it all again, every back-breaking inch of the route, with a twitchy passenger who flinched when I turned too sharply, and got angry if I asked a question he considered 'judge-mental'. By the time we'd made it to the Greek border, I was sick as a dog, probably from a 'local' bottle of Bulgarian spring water.

What was going on?

I'd spent months visualizing the journey to Romania across seven countries, despite having never left the UK before. The trip to Romania went smoothly, as if we were blessed.

In Thessaloniki, I decided that we should cut the trip short and take the most direct route back home. With Mount Olympus in temptation's reach, I headed in the opposite direction.

Later that day, I watched the sun sink over the Ionian Sea from the pretty port town of Igounmenitsa where we waited for the ferry to Brindisi, on the 'heel' of Italy. We were parked outside an Italian restaurant when Sven went into one of his paranoid rants. By now I was scared; he was a ticking time bomb waiting to explode. As I sat trying to ignore Sven, completing my notes about the day's drive across the mountains of Greece, he lunged at me.

Regrettably, my knee-jerk reaction was to release several days of pent-up frustration into two or three right crosses to his face. Later I apologized from the bottom of my heart and tried to look after him like an injured bird that had fallen from its nest.

I decided that I would use all of my emergency cash to fly Sven home from Naples. There, he seemed to forgive me, and apologized for his behaviour—he was the first to admit what a fool he'd been for stopping his medication. Still, it had been an adventure, and for that he thanked me. He waved goodbye and turned into the departure lounge, out of my life forever.

I never saw a penny from Sven for the petrol, for the food he ate, nothing. Nor did I receive a penny towards his flight home, for which he'd promised to pay half once he was home. So it turned out that I'd not only chauffeured the man across Europe, but paid for the privilege as well. Lessons learned!

After leaving Naples, I explored Rome, ventured north to enjoy the delights of Pisa, including its famous Leaning Tower, before eventually leaving Italy via the Italian Riviera, stopping at Villefranche-sur-Mer beyond the French border.

It was here that the final disaster happened. While I swam in the deep blue Mediterranean and walked along the beautiful beach—gone for only forty minutes—my car was robbed of absolutely everything I had. I stood in the midday sun, wearing shorts, shirt, and sandals, carrying a bumbag with just a few francs, passport, keys and sun cream. Everything else had gone, including the diary I'd been keeping since Naples. Thank goodness I'd posted the previous entries back home.

I managed to cancel my credit cards and open a temporary bank account in Marseille so I could have some money wired over. The hassles continued for the remainder of the trip, but I finally crossed the English Channel for the six-hour drive home.

I had been gone for less than a month, yet it felt as though I'd been away for a year. I arrived back a completely different person.

Reflections

I sat up in the makeshift bed in the temple. All was still and quiet. I pondered the two different aspects of the trip. It was all adventure to me, but the outbound journey was remarkably smoother than the return journey, when really, being an easier route, it should have been the other way around.

I thought of the guide's wise words earlier that afternoon, about holding a thought on the screen of your mind for a sustained period, and causing the Universe to stir as it brings that very thing into your reality.

THE OUTBOUND METHOD: I held every aspect of that outbound journey on the screen of my mind, for a sustained period.

THE OUTBOUND RESULT: We enjoyed a blessed journey where everything fell into place. We were always at the right place at the right time, and like magic, people, places and circumstances danced to our tune.

THE RETURN JOURNEY METHOD: I did not give much thought to the return journey. Sure, I planned a route, and I circled a few places of interest on the map, but I did not imagine visiting those locations, I gave no thought to what it might 'feel' like to drive into Turkey, for example.

THE RETURN JOURNEY RESULT: I'd been attacked by a gang of thugs trying to smash their way into my car, stranded overnight on a cold beach, refused entry into Turkey, had the car grind to a halt thanks to the wrong fuel being added, had the car break down in Sofia due to engine flooding, ended up in the wrong country which was in a state of civil war, been poisoned by Bulgarian water, punched my travelling companion before sending him home, and then been robbed of everything except my shirt and shorts in the south of France!

I decided to focus more from that day forth on holding images on the screen of my mind that matched the journey I wanted to undertake. I would start by applying this method to my trek, as I aimed for the summit of this sacred mountain.

Rejoining My Guide

My brain had worked overtime remembering the Romanian expedition, but my body had lain still and felt rejuvenated.

A gentle knock on the door. "Your supper is ready, sir," said a temple worker, opening the door a little. "Please, follow me to eat."

I wasted no time in following him out of my room, passing numerous open areas filled with the heady aroma of joss sticks and incense cones. In the eating area, I was pleased to see Pierce in the corner waiting for me.

"Are you suitably rested?" he asked, with the inflection of a classically trained actor.

"Kind of," I replied. "I've been thinking about what you told me today. Are you joining me?" I added, practically sitting on the floor at the low table.

"Thank you, but I have eaten already," he replied, gently placing his hand on his stomach. "You say you have given thought to the advice I gave you today?"

"Yes. I was thinking back to a key event in my life, and how for part of the trip I'd thought a lot about…"

"And the list?" he interrupted with a smile.

I took a mouthful of rice as I considered what he was asking me, and washed it down with a sweet fruit juice.

"Ah. You mean the list of things I want?"

Pierce raised an eyebrow, but continued to smile. "Indeed, I asked you to draw up a list of things that you want to have or experience in your life."

"No," I said, "I haven't got around to that yet."

"Ah," he replied, the smile slowly dropping from his sun-kissed face, replaced instead by a look of sorrow. "You didn't…get 'around to it' you say."

He pulled out a walking stick from beside his seat, and leant on it as he stood. It came up to his chest, so it was more of a staff than a walking stick.

I wasn't prepared for the next moment.

To my shock and amazement, he raised his staff as if to strike me, his eyebrows joining together in a scowl. He doubled the volume of his voice as he loudly repeated himself.

"You didn't get… 'around to it'?"

Before I could move a muscle or utter a single word, his angry face relaxed, and he raised the staff until it was comfortably over his shoulder. He smiled and opened the door.

"In that case I shall wait for you by your quarters, and help you in any way I can," he said. "You enjoy the rest of your food, and drink plenty of fluid. I will be waiting."

With that he turned and swished out of the door into the dusk. I sat for a second, staring at the closed door. Silence.

Later in my room, I sat on the low bed with my backpack contents around me, and a notepad and pencil at the ready. Pierce preferred to stand, pacing back and forth like a bored tiger in a small zoo enclosure.

I tapped my pencil against my chin, and looked pensively at the floor. "Sorry, Pierce," I said. "My mind's gone blank."

Pierce stopped his pacing, and leaned on his staff with both hands in front of him.

"It is to be expected—for you have never used your mind as it was truly intended—until now," he said. "Just write down a few things that you want. What would your life look like if it were perfect right now? What would be different?"

My mind remained blank. What would I want if I could have anything?

"Well," I began, "I don't want to keep struggling financially any more. That would be a start. And I guess I…"

"No. Stop! I did not ask you want you *do not want*." Pierce lowered his voice and appealed to me sincerely, as if it really mattered to him. "I want you to tell me what you *do* want!"

He began to pace again, and took the persona of a school teacher.

"I will tell you what. Today is the last day that you will talk of what you do *not* want, for if you hold the image in your mind of what you do not want, you must bring that into your life as surely as night follows day. Good or bad, the Law of Creation never stops working; it will create in this world exactly what you think about most of the time.

"If you are thinking *lack* of money, then you will create more *lack* of money. If you are thinking of an *abundance* of money, then you will create an *abundance* of money."

He took my pad and pencil from me. "For today only, let us exorcize these demons. Let us discuss what you *do not* want. But you must not give those thoughts any power; try not to *feel* the feelings usually associated with them. Let us instead, simply write them down."

He got me to tear seven sheets of paper from my pad and draw a vertical line down the centre of each sheet. He then asked me to write a title at the top of each sheet of paper: Physical, Mind, Financial, Spiritual, Interaction, Charitable and Gratitude.

"Good, then we shall begin. Pick a sheet; which one have you chosen?"

"Physical," I said, opting for what I considered an easy choice.

"All right," he replied, looking very serious for the first time since the dining room. "To the left of that centre line, write down something that you do not want that refers to your body or physical self."

"That's easy. I don't want a beer belly!"

Pierce raised an eyebrow. "Then write it down. What else?"

"I don't want a stinking cold like I have now, and I don't want to be so unfit, my legs and back aching as they do now. I don't want to be weak."

"Good," the guide said, walking around and looking over my shoulder at the pad. "Don't want: beer belly, cold, to be unfit, to be weak. Great. Now to the right of the line, write down what you *want*. So, next to 'beer belly' write 'flat stomach' and so on, until you have finished the list."

I did this, and then he asked me to tear the paper in two, right down the centre dividing line.

He then asked me to screw up the side about what I *didn't* want, before adopting the guise of a children's party conjuror, hovering his hand over the screwed up paper. When he moved his quivering hand, the paper was gone. As a former magician myself, I knew how he did the trick, but it still brought a smile to my face and took the seriousness out of the lesson I was being given.

"Take up your pencil," he said, "and write the following at the top of that remaining piece of paper: 'I feel so happy and thankful, now that I have'... Good. Now read everything on the paper," said Pierce with a huge nod and a grin.

"I see what you're doing, it's like setting a goal and..."

"No, no, no. Read it *aloud!*"

"Oh. 'I feel so happy and thankful, now that I have a flat stomach, a healthy immune system, peak fitness, great strength and muscle tone'."

"Again!"

'I feel so happy and thankful, now that I have a flat stomach, a healthy immune system, peak fitness, with great strength and muscle tone'.

"Again," he said, raising both his voice, and his staff to the heavens, "with *feeling!*"

'I feel *so* happy and *so* thankful, now that I have a flat stomach, a healthy immune system, peak physical fitness, with great strength and muscle tone'! I spoke with a new-found confidence.

"Good, good. Now if you said that every day, and 'felt' that every day, you would cause that thing you thought about to be created in this world. You might feel inspired to take up jogging or yoga, and find that beer would be the last drink you desired after training.

"As your stretching and exercise became more common, you might find yourself drawn to the right foods, and as your stomach fat lessened, and your healthy diet fought the colds off by boosting the immune system, you might feel better and better.

"As you mentioned being happy and thankful, now that you had a flatter stomach, a healthier immune system, and improved fitness, you would keep attracting more and more things to you that would make that come true. Like a magic magnet, by holding the thought and then the feeling, you create your own destiny. You will look back, and I promise, be amazed at the slimmer, healthier, fitter, stronger person that confidently smiles back at you from the mirror.

"It all started when you made that list, because you put that thought out there. By thinking those thoughts caused by writing down your list, you set the wheels in motion to achieve that. All you have to do is read that list aloud every morning to remind yourself of how good those things feel, and take action as the circumstances appear in your life.

"So if the next day a leaflet arrives in the mail for a new gymnasium that has opened, join it! If a friend mentions how great they feel after drinking green tea instead of coffee at breakfast, take the hint and try some green tea!"

I folded that torn piece of paper and placed it in my pocket. Then I asked, "Why Mind, Financial, Spiritual, Interaction, Charitable and Gratitude? What is that all about?"

"My friend, Physical, Mental, Financial, Spiritual, Interaction, Charitable, and Gratitude are the very pillars of your life. If we neglect to maintain any of these, then the building they support—your life—will quickly be in ruins."

We spent the remainder of that evening in deep conversation. Pierce went through each of these titles in detail before asking me to write down what I didn't want in each area of my life. He then asked me to rephrase each point into a phrase saying what I *did* want. As before he asked me to tear the strip in two, keep the positive side, throw away the negative, and write the "I am so happy and thankful now that…" affirmation at the top of the 'want' list.

By the time we'd finished, it must have been 11 p.m. Despite my enthusiasm, I'd walked many miles that day, and by the time I'd finished my final list I was struggling to keep my eyes open.

"You have done well," Pierce said, speaking to me like a parent tucking a young child up after a bedtime story. "You will sleep very well tonight; you will sleep deeply, and soundly, deeper than you have slept in a very long time."

Had I known what was coming tomorrow, I wouldn't have slept a wink.

YOUR TURN

I found the exercise I completed that night to be a great starting point in turning my life around. It really worked for me. I've shared this with others before writing this book, and it's worked for them too. The great secret of creation that Pierce had started to share with me that day works for everybody on planet Earth, regardless of age, sex, colour, or nationality.

Simply do as I did: write down on the left of the page all that annoying stuff you *don't want* to have in your life anymore, then re-write it on the right of the page in a way that explains what you *do want*.

So in 'Interaction', which deals with the people and relationships in your life, you might write on the left of the page, 'I don't want a husband that never supports me in anything I do, and mocks my new ideas and dreams.' Then, to the right of that statement write, 'I want a husband who supports me in everything I do, who encourages me in my new ideas and dreams.'

You're saying pretty much the same thing, but you're saying it in a positive way, and focusing like a laser on exactly what you *want*.

So, when the list is complete for that subject, all that remains is to add the sentence at the start: 'I feel so happy and thankful, now that I have...' and word it in the present tense, so the above reads: 'I feel so happy and thankful, now that I have a husband who supports me in everything I do, who encourages me in my new ideas and dreams.'

Tear or cut each page in two, and throw away the negative (I don't want) side.

Finally, it might be a good idea to copy all of the seven 'I want' lists to a single powerful 'Wish List'. I've left a blank one of those on the website for you too.

Put the list somewhere you'll see it every day, or keep it on your person if you want to keep your dreams private. However, put it somewhere you'll see it often – your wallet, handbag, purse, near your car keys, somewhere obvious.

Forget that part of the list you threw away. From this day forth, you think only of the things you *want* in life, and if you find yourself thinking about something you *don't* want ('I'm sick of being poor') quickly throw that ball into the air of your mind, and hit it out of the park! Think instead of what you *do* want ('I want to be wealthy') and then think about it as if it's already happened ('I'm so happy now that I can travel with my loved ones to exotic locations three times a year').

Why not go and print off those sheets right now? You could do the exercise now, as soon as you've finished this chapter.

Be the person who never puts obstacles in the way, and never puts things off because they're a little tired, or because their TV show is starting in a moment. It takes just a few minutes, and you will be so happy deep inside when you have completed the exercise and finished this chapter.

By completing the exercise, you will have started the creation process. Just by identifying your goals and imagining having them in the present tense, you will have started the process of creation right away. Not in a week, or a month, or a year—now, today. The wheels will be in motion as you finish the list, and when you wake up in the morning. Just don't doubt it for a second; read your list before breakfast to remind yourself, and allow yourself to feel excited for the life that just changed its direction and for the things now coming your way.

Have your list ready for when you start Chapter Two tomorrow, because what the guide revealed next was not only astonishing, but *will* have a profound effect on your life.

"Take rest; a field that has rested gives a bountiful crop."
— PUBLIUS OVIDIUS NASO *(43 BC–AD 18), ROMAN POET*

Relax

I woke the next day, a quiet rain tickling the door to my temple room. It brought with it a cool, refreshing breeze that cleared the air and allowed me to inhale deeply. The cool air in my lungs felt better than water to a dry, thirsty throat.

Rising from the makeshift bed, my legs stiff from the previous day's climb, I tried to stretch my back, which was as taut as a strongman's bow.

Despite the aching back and legs, I was keen to cover my blisters and start walking as quickly as possible. The thought of what this day might hold filled me with excitement. Not only should I gain some altitude, but I might also attain a little more insight from my guide.

Pierce didn't show up for breakfast that morning, but I found him waiting by the temple entrance, fully kitted up, and looking as fresh as the morning dew.

"Good morning," I said, as he nodded to the gatekeeper to remove the beam that secured the large wooden door. "Sorry I missed you at breakfast."

"The fault was all mine," he replied with a warm smile. "I rose much earlier and drank green tea before some meditation with my friends."

"You meditate?"

"I certainly do," he said, scratching his white beard with a playful look in his eyes. "I certainly do."

What followed was a thorough check of my equipment, a look at my blisters, and a detailed explanation of the route we would take that day. This guy was good.

Onwards and Upwards

Within an hour of leaving the temple, we had gained a lot of height and finally swapped the humid, almost tropical surrounds for a highland landscape. From now on, the path would be more barren and rock strewn, until we crossed the snow line in a day or two.

My back held up for half an hour before becoming sore again. As I twisted to ease my aching back, my leg also began to niggle. I coughed and spluttered and was forever wiping my nose that day, but I was also pleased the headache had gone; my head felt decluttered, like a home after a thorough spring clean.

Pierce kept ahead of me that morning, like a pacemaker training an athlete. Frustratingly, every time I dug deep and was about to catch him up, he would somehow slip into a higher gear and leave me behind.

I couldn't quite fathom why he was doing it. The last mountain I had climbed had been Kilimanjaro, where the Tanzanian guides walked painfully slowly, saying *"pole, pole"* (poley, poley) meaning "slowly, slowly". This made the early stages of climbing the world's highest freestanding mountain very annoying, but the guides knew what they were doing.

Kilimanjaro is 19,344 feet high, and I chose the Lemosho route for my expedition, which starts further down the mountain than the more popular tourist routes. This meant the 'height gain' was greater from start to finish, and so the key to success was to walk very slowly, and to let your body get used to the thin air. I suffered only very minor altitude sickness on the day I summited, due largely to the slow pace over the week's climb. *"Pole, pole"* helped me to conquer the highest mountain in Africa, even if I did find it ten times slower than my usual pace.

So why was Pierce so keen to dash off whenever I caught him up?

Perhaps I was over-analyzing it; maybe he just wanted to be on his own for a little while that day. That didn't make it any less annoying. I had hoped to chat to him about my new goals.

It wasn't until we stopped for lunch that second day that we began to talk some more.

A Mind-Stretching Lunch

Sheltered between two large rock formations, Pierce ducked out of the cool breeze. When I joined him he clapped his hands with delight, still looking as fresh as before we had started walking.

"Well done," he said. "You've done remarkably well to make it here for lunch. Sit with me. Take the weight off your feet and enjoy a well-earned rest."

Pierce made me feel very relaxed. I'd known him for just a day and a half, yet settling down beside him was like joining a lifelong friend. It was most unexpected, and very pleasant.

"Thanks," I said. "I'm still struggling to breathe a bit, and still coughing and wiping my nose every few minutes, but other than that, I'm OK." I decided not to mention the blisters, aching back and throbbing legs. Flopping down opposite Pierce, sheltered from the wind, it was good to finally talk.

"I've been thinking a lot this morning, Pierce," I continued, "about the things on my list, about the things I really want."

"What else?" he replied.

"How do you mean?"

"I mean, apart from those desires you scribed on paper last night, what else have you thought about?"

"Oh, the usual," I said, peeling a banana. "Home, the kids, what my wife would think of it here, work, money. I've also been distracted by the views, Pierce—some amazing sights. That view when we left the forest, the one with…"

"Interesting," he interrupted. "Interesting that you mention being 'distracted', it's good that you realize this."

I nodded, but managed to look puzzled at the same time.

"When you form a clear image of the life you want, on the screen of your mind, you must keep it there."

"How do you mean? For how long?"

"Well, ideally you should sit quietly at least twice a day, and ponder these images. Perhaps you do this early in the morning, while your home is quiet, before your spouse or children break the silence. Perhaps again at night, before bed—which is particularly good as your creative mind will replay those images as you sleep—to reinforce your positive intentions.

"Whatever the time of day, you should sit in a quiet place where you will not be disturbed, and try to imagine what it would be like to have the things you want, right now, as if you already had the person you desire, or the children, or the job, or the home or the car, whatever it is that you seek. You can have, be, or do, anything your heart truly desires."

I waited for him to say 'within reason', but he didn't.

He really believed you could become the person you wanted to become, own the things that you wanted to own, and do anything you set your mind to. He seemed so 'matter of fact' about it that I found myself yearning to learn more.

"I think I'd find it hard to focus on one desire for any length of time, without my mind drifting," I confessed.

He nodded, and then closed his eyes, inhaling deeply through his nose. With his eyes still closed, a smile of contentment slowly formed on his glowing face. His eyes opened, and the smile remained.

"The only true way to change your *future*," he said, "is to learn how to use your mind correctly in the *present*.

"In order to use your mind as it was intended, you're going to have to learn how to quieten the mind: get rid of the noise, the internal chatter, and the constant distractions fighting for your attention.

"The first step is relaxation. Through relaxation and correct breathing, you can quieten the mind, ready to transform your life."

He leaned back so that his back was against the rock face, with his head looking skyward.

"Do you see those clouds?" he asked. "The ones above us?"

"I do."

"Remember them."

I nodded.

"Notice how they are not in any hurry. Notice how they are not holding back either. They just..." he paused, looked away from the sky above and straight into my eyes. "They just *are*."

He raised both eyebrows, waiting for a response, and then smiled warmly. He continued, turning his attention back to the clouds. "When you enter a state of deep relaxation, meditation even, you just... are. You will understand once you are meditating, my friend."

I laughed at the mere mention of such a notion.

"Me? Meditating?" I decided to be completely honest. Pierce made me feel that way, as if I could tell him anything. "To be truthful, I've tried to meditate before, and my mind just kept wandering. I couldn't do it."

"Oh, that happens to everyone to begin with," he said, pointing at the clouds again. "The trick is to just let those thoughts drift by the screen of your mind, just as you watch the clouds drift by over your head. They are not spoiling your view of that beautiful sky, they were not invited by you, they are just there, passing by. They just *are*. Watch them float by for a second, know they are drifting by, and refocus on the sky, or in meditation, on the screen of your mind."

"I see. If only it were that easy," I said.

"Do you doubt me?" the guide said, leaning on his stick to stand.

"No, no, heck no. I just don't think I'd find it that easy," I replied, concerned by him rising to his feet, in case I'd offended him.

He wasn't offended. It was simply time to move on. Lunch was over. He adjusted his old haversack, and gestured for me to follow him up the rocky slope.

Higher and Higher

"I find you puzzling, my friend," he said, talking forward while I walked behind, his voice dulled by the cold breeze. "You seem to have made your mind up that you cannot relax, cannot meditate, and yet I tell you that with my guidance, you will be able to do this very quickly and easily."

I jogged to catch him up, and walked to his right, and this time he did not pick up the pace. If anything he slowed down.

"You see, when you read a book, and you are momentarily seeing images of people walking together in your mind, that is meditation. Your body is relaxed, and for a moment, you are not aware of the world around you. If I were to say to you now, that a moment ago, you were not aware of your big toe on your left foot, I would be correct. But now, you *are* aware of the big toe on your left foot, are you not? Is it comfortable? Perhaps you want to wiggle your toes right now!

"Yet, a moment ago, you were not aware of it, were you? When you read a book, it is a form of meditation. When you watch your moving pictures, you are engrossed in the story and transported to the time and era of that show, are you not?"

I found it odd how Pierce spoke sometimes. "Moving pictures?" I asked with a sarcastic tone to my voice.

"Yes, yes. Television, the cinema, you knew what I meant. I am old, I will call the radio the wireless for eternity," he said, laughing. "But do you understand me? When I talk of meditation, I do not necessarily talk of burning incense, with you sitting down with your legs tied in a knot around your head. I just mean the ability to *relax*. To shut off the 'outside world', and switch on the 'inside world'; it's like waking from a dream that is bearable, to find yourself in a reality that is paradise."

"Cool," I said. "I like that. I'm just not sure I…"

"Remember what we spoke of yesterday, my dear friend. Remember to keep an open mind, and to *believe*. I can easily teach you during our time together, how to do these things. All I need from you is a little faith. For you to believe in yourself, and to believe the things I share with you, for I speak only the truth. A truth that has echoed through the centuries to only the few that would listen.

"A wise man once said, 'Faith is to believe what you do not yet see; the reward for this faith is to see what you believe'. I happen to agree with Saint Augustine in this regard."

I nodded, as the sound of rushing water drew near. "You're a wise man, Pierce, and I'm grateful for you sharing this with me."

"Not at all, the pleasure is all mine," he said. The path turned a corner to reveal a rope bridge crossing a fast flowing stream. "I want to share this with anyone who will listen to me. For it will surely transform their world, and the lives of all the souls those people come into contact with."

The Rope Bridge

My eyes widened at the sight of such fast flowing water, smashing through the ravine as it had done for millennia. The bridge looked secure enough, and so I walked onto it as Pierce held back to pick up something he'd dropped.

I leaned on the old blackened rope and walked to the centre of the rickety crossing, breathing in the fresh misty air kicked up by the rapids below. For a moment my breathlessness disappeared. I closed my eyes and inhaled deeply. With my eyes closed I could sense more—the sound of the rushing water, the mineral smell of the place, the taste of moisture in the air, and the smooth feel of aged rope against the palm of my hands.

"Good, I see the student is listening to the master," said Pierce, walking onto the bridge with a stick in each hand. One was his walking stick, the other was an old muddy and broken stick, about a foot long. "Trying a little meditation perhaps?"

"No," I corrected him with a big smile. "Just taking in the moment."

"Ah," he said. "Good. To appreciate one's surroundings is a fantastic practice. To send out vibes of gratitude into the Universe is a powerful thing. Do you recall yesterday? The very basics of the Law of Creation? We attract into our lives the very things we think about most often. The very *feeling* we vibrate at, attracts things to us, be they material goods, people, or experiences, which vibrate at the same level. It is so, whether we like it or not. By *feeling* appreciation or gratitude in the moment, as you just did, you send out a powerful message that will bring good things to you. You mark my words."

He smiled, walking over the rope bridge to join me at the centre.

"Perhaps we should talk more about gratitude another time. What I wanted to address now is relaxation, and in particular, the little doubts that seem to be creeping in about whether you can meditate, or indeed, whether this knowledge is for you."

He rested his staff against the side of the bridge, and held the small muddy stick in both hands, his arms raised like a Native American Chief offering a pipe to a distinguished guest.

"The truth is that anything is possible. You of all people should know that. This doubt inside of you is a negative emotion, is it not?"

He raised an eyebrow, and I nodded, the stick still held aloft before me.

"It makes your heart heavy, it tightens your chest, yes? We must learn how to clean these negative emotions, to adjust your vibration from that place of doubt, to that place of possibility.

"Now, observe this old broken walking stick, tossed away upstream no doubt, many years ago. Let us pretend for a moment that the covering of dirt and grime on this stick represents the many layers of negative emotions you have built up over the years, regarding a certain subject. Take meditation, for example; you told me earlier that you had tried it, and could not do it, that your mind kept wandering? Those doubts are the mud and grit upon this very stick. Here, take it from me, my arms begin to ache." I took it from him, holding the stick in front of me as he had, using both hands.

"You see," he continued, "negative emotions can take many forms. We have spoken of doubt, but there is more dirt on the stick. See the thick clay-like substance on the end?"

"Yes."

"Let us pretend that clay is 'worry'—where you have worried about not being able to meditate. Do you see that almost black dirt? Let us pretend that is jealousy—perhaps you were unknowingly jealous of those who could meditate when you tried it before. Your uncertainty, your anguish, and your envy—all of these are forms of negative emotion that do not serve you well, my friend.

"The good news is, you can wash away these futile emotions as easily as we can wash away the filth upon this old stick."

With the speed of a young featherweight boxer, Pierce snatched the stick from my hands. Before I could even flinch, he spun, leant back and threw the stick high into the air over the bridge.

"Look, look!" he pointed with his long finger. "See the stick?"

"Yes," I replied, as it hit the water and was quickly carried out of sight by the raging torrent. "Can you still see it?"

"Not really, Pierce. I mean, I think I…"

"No matter. Come, let us cross this bridge and pause for a moment beneath that overhang on the other side." He picked up his staff, and crossed the bridge at a pace.

When I caught him up, he was starting to sit down.

"Sit, sit," he said. "I want you to close your eyes for the briefest of moments.

"If a thought drifts into your mind, just let it be. Like a cloud crossing the sky, you see it, watch for a moment knowing it drifts on by, and look again beyond it, to the stillness of the sky."

He breathed in with me, much slower than I, and as he exhaled through his mouth, he made a slow and audible 'har' sound. We did this for a few minutes, breathing in through the nose for perhaps four seconds, a slight pause, then breathing out through the mouth for as long as eight seconds.

I found just thinking of my breathing helped my mind to stop wandering. I was aware of the cool air going in through my nostrils and filling my lungs, and I was noticing the out breath and copying the guide's breathy 'har' sound.

After just a minute or two I found myself in a very relaxed state. My body became as comfortable as the most indulgent weekend lie-in; you know the feeling, when you plan to rise early but wake to the sound of rain lashing against the windows, and decide to turn off the alarm and have another hour with the soft, warm duvet wrapped around you. That's how my body felt.

My mind, on the other hand, was quite alert. It was still receptive, listening to Pierce, and ready to conjure up the image he spoke of, on the screen of my mind, while my body switched into 'autopilot' in a blissful state of relaxation.

Pierce gently leaned forward towards my ear, and spoke in a whisper.

"Now, think back to that stick, when you held it on the bridge."

I tried my best to imagine what he described.

"Now, the dirt on the stick was all that negativity, yes? Then we tossed it into that fast flowing river, yes? Well, we can now only imagine where it is right now. It is, as I speak, travelling downstream and as it does so, the dirt is being washed away.

"Imagine that. Imagine the negative emotions being washed away by the cleansing, pure waters of this ancient river.

"As the stick continues downstream to gentler waters, it becomes cleaner, and cleaner, and cleaner. By the time it floats atop that wider expanse of water near the mouth of the river, it is almost completely clean.

"As the fresh water gives way to salt water, and the river becomes the ocean, the stick is as white as a bleached bone. The negativity has gone, and only pure white goodness remains.

"Imagine that, and feel grateful as that white stick bobs along on the ocean towards the warming sun that lowers on the horizon."

I visualized everything he said, but began to drift towards sleep with the final image of the clean stick bobbing on the ocean towards the sunset. "You're making me tired." I smiled with a yawn. "Can I open my eyes now?"

"Indeed you can." He seemed pleased that I'd done as he asked, that I'd tried to use my mind in this way.

"Now," he said, "we could not see the stick once it had hit the water, but we could imagine it well enough, could we not? We could imagine those negative emotions being cleaned away.

"What if I told you that you could use that imagery as often as you like, to calm your mind and rid yourself of negative thoughts whenever the need arose?"

He rose to his feet and nodded towards the steep path ahead.

"Come, let us complete today's walking, for the temple is towards the top of the path ahead."

To the Temple

I felt a strange sense of relief that we would be stopping at a temple again that night. I had enjoyed the previous evening's peaceful shelter, but had assumed it was a 'one-off' treat, prior to a week of camping in tents.

The walk from the river crossing was arduous. What I thought would be a strenuous half-hour ascent, became a two-hour scramble on scree. At each false summit after false summit, Pierce encouraged me on with promises of being 'almost there'.

When I glimpsed the beginnings of a small village, I became unexpectedly exhausted. The last two hours had knocked the stuffing out of me.

I hadn't coughed in some time, which was good but that small improvement was overshadowed by my streaming nose, blisters, and my aching back and legs. I was getting used to the breathlessness, but the combination of my personal challenges and the pace of the last few hours had taken its toll.

A pleasant aroma of cooking filled my nostrils as we entered the village. The rumble of my stomach momentarily took my mind off my eagerness to locate the temple and fall onto any kind of bed or mattress.

The village was different from the last. It was obvious that fewer 'visitors' came this way, because the people were reacting as if a stranger had walked into their house unannounced. Mothers appeared from nowhere to grab their children, and scold them for looking at us, ushering them quickly inside their homes.

Small fires burned outside, just inches from the main thoroughfare, with clay pots bubbling away, and thick pungent smoke blowing across our path.

The houses here were built slightly better than the last village, which seemed odd considering we were higher and more remote. Through the patches of thick smoke, I saw that some dwellings had shutters, all painted the same dirty orange colour. Not all of the buildings were thatched this time; one or two had more solid roofs constructed of a clay-like tile.

A small group of young men assembled behind us. They appeared to be suspicious of us. As the gang began to grow and slowly follow us through the village, Pierce quickened his pace and looked over his shoulder to check that I was catching him up.

"The people of this village are simple folk. They mean well, but are generally a discouraged bunch. I always sense anger when I pass this way; it is like the people feel they have been 'wronged' somehow. It is a shame, but it has been this way for at least a hundred years."

"Why?" I asked, spotting the temple after leaving another bank of smoke.

"Because they choose to predominantly think angry, suspicious and discouraging thoughts, my friend."

With that, we arrived at the temple entrance, and not before time. The crowd that followed had been joined by women and children, and was close to becoming a curious mob.

A Welcome Retreat

The entrance had two simple pillars either side of an arched doorway. Its walls were covered in a curious orangey clay.

It was very plain, just a few strange symbols over the large wooden doors, which shook as I thumped the metal knocker on Pierce's command.

Some rattling and scraping occurred from inside, and the doors creaked loudly as they slowly parted to reveal our host.

A short man in pale orange robes looked me up and down inquisitively. "English? American? Can I help?" he asked in a slow, deliberate manner.

I glanced sideways at Pierce, but he was busy watching the murmuring crowd behind us.

"Yes," I replied. "Do you have rooms?"

The man smiled, bowed, and beckoned us forward. "You are most welcome."

Any tension disappeared the moment we were safely inside and the temple entrance slammed shut and locked. I peeked through the thin gap between the doors to see the crowd disperse and go about their business.

Pierce spoke in a hushed tone, close to my ear. "I have some business of my own to attend to, my friend. Go rest a while and you will see me soon enough."

I was happy to follow the temple worker to my quarters, and longed for an afternoon nap.

I saw more people inside this temple. Some were sitting alone in contemplation, others were carrying firewood or food, and some were spreading the aroma of incense in one way or another, while quietly chanting. The scent was pleasant, and different from the last temple, although I tried not to inhale too deeply for fear of triggering my cough again.

Dodging people and ducking to avoid the long orange flags that fluttered between buildings, I made it to my room. The temple worker bowed, smiled and turned away into the warren of alleyways between buildings.

The room was very similar to the last one, which was great because I'd slept well the night before. The only slight differences were the position of the bed, this time closer to the window so I could write my journal from the bed if I wanted to, and a small, simple cupboard to the right side of the bed. "Good enough for a few books and an alarm clock," I thought.

Although the room was very basic, it felt like indulgent luxury after the ground covered during the hike that day.

After removing boots and two pairs of socks I barely had time to tend to my blisters when the bed beckoned. I let out a sigh as I lowered myself onto the straw mattress beneath the window. Lying horizontal made my breathing more difficult, but I was too tired to care.

With increasingly heavy eyelids, I began to reflect on the day's events.

The words of the wise guide drifted back to me. They crept into my subconscious like morning fog drifting over dew-covered fields.

"The only true way to change your *future*, is to learn how to use your mind correctly in the *present*."

In that place between waking and sleeping, I saw Pierce smile broadly in my mind's eye.

"To shut off the 'outside world' and switch on the 'inside world' is like waking from a dream that is bearable, to find yourself in a reality that is paradise."

I grinned as I remembered our encounter after crossing the bridge that day. Sitting still with Pierce, as he described the muddy stick travelling downstream, felt good.

The breathing technique—deep slow breaths, in through the nose, out through the mouth. So easy and yet so effective.

As I lay there, still unable to get a full breath due to the altitude, I reflected on the importance of being able to breathe properly, and how few people actually do.

I had learned this as part of my training to become a stuntman.

The Drama of Drama School

A person training to become a professional stunt performer has to cover a wide variety of skills. Not just black belt or instructor standards in martial arts, fencing, swimming, high diving, sub-aqua, horse riding, climbing, trampolining, skydiving and so forth. They also have to join the actors' union, and gain around 60 days of 'on set' experience.

In order to join the actors' union, I trained as an actor at the New Era Academy of Speech and Drama, London. That sounds quite grand, doesn't it? It wasn't; it was a 'distance learning' affair, with a number of smaller drama schools in major towns and cities across the UK affiliated to the New Era Academy in London.

Twice a week, I would make my way across the city of Nottingham to the tutor's private home, and learn one on one how to become a thespian!

I'll always cringe at the memory of learning a passage from *The Lion, the Witch and the Wardrobe*; having to speak the words of the young Edmund as he greedily seeks more Turkish Delight was pitiful. Shouting out with gusto as the Snow Queen was even worse!

But it served its purpose, and at least one thing I took away from those rainy afternoons has served me well. One of the first lessons my acting coach taught me was how to breathe properly. I had given the matter little thought, if any, and yet what I learned surprised me.

What I'd been doing for as long as I could remember was breathing from high in my chest. For example, if somebody told me to 'breathe in' as a teenager, I would suck my tummy in to look thinner. What trained actors do is to breathe from their stomach area first, then the chest. This technique, known as intercostal diaphragmatic breathing, allows an actor to recite a long line from a Shakespearean play.

So now, if someone asks me to hold my breath, they'll notice that instead of my stomach sucking in, it actually bloats out as I fill my lungs with air.

Try it. Place the flat of your hand on your belly and take a deep breath. Your hand should rise as the lungs fill with air, like a balloon inflating inside a bird cage, pushing the bars (the ribs) out as the balloon inflates.

If your hand sinks in, this means you're breathing incorrectly. Don't worry, a lot of people breathe that way.

The beauty of intercostal breathing is that with a little practice, you can learn to do this very easily. Just become aware of how you breathe, and place your hand on your stomach as you do so. Your hand rises with the 'in breath', and sinks on the 'out breath', as all the air is expelled from the lungs.

You will find that the brain soon rewires itself and begins to breathe this way all by itself. Then, for the rest of your life, you can enjoy greater lung volume, making sure you are fit and healthy.

It allows me to calm down before a big stunt if I start to feel nervous as I wait for the countdown to "Action!" It also allows me to hold my breath underwater for long periods of time, or whilst performing dangerous fire stunts.

Not bad, for someone who was never athletic. It wasn't until I was about 13 that I made an impulsive decision to do something sporty.

| The Great North Run |

Before that, I wasn't sporty at all. I found football and cricket boring, and never made the effort. I was always one of the last people to be chosen at school for a team. Remember the last four stragglers that were always left? The thin weak child, the one with thick spectacles on, the goofy kid, the soft computer nerd? I was tall and skinny, and blessed with two left feet.

I did enjoy rugby, which was unusual considering my thoughts on sport in general, but I could run like the wind and also enjoyed a bit of 'rough and tumble'. Unfortunately, my school didn't have a rugby team, only football and cricket, so I didn't look forward to sports lessons.

One part of the school calendar I particularly loathed was the dreaded 'cross country' season. Looking back, it was probably only a couple of miles, if that, but at the time it felt like a marathon. Although I could run the 100 metres very quickly on Sports Day, I was never any good at distance running. I always ended up at the back with my reject friends from the team selection. There I would be, walking, nursing a stitch, chatting to the student with the thick specs, the goofy child, and the pale wimpy computer nerd.

A strange thing happened one day when I was 13 years old. Some nerdy friends and I were in the school hall after an assembly, when some of the school's 'sports heroes' were boasting about a forthcoming sporting event—the Great North Run. The half marathon, which began in 1981, has become one of the world's most popular races, winding its way from the heart of Newcastle to the finishing line in South Shields, some 13.1 miles away.

In the school hall, as the sporty types bragged about their latest challenge, the Great North Run, I made a chance remark. "What's the big deal? Anyone can train to run really slow for miles and miles." Childish, I know. I was 13. The sports hunks turned and mocked me. "Well, *we* could train Curtis, but *you* couldn't. You can't even do a lap of the school field in cross country!"

My nerdy friends came to my rescue. "He could do it if he wanted to, couldn't you, Curtis? So could we. We just have better things to do."

"Like what?!" growled the sports heroes.

Before my friends admitted to playing Donkey Kong or Pac-Man for kicks, I cut in and tried to save face. "Get us a few forms to enter this race, and all three of us will do the Great North Run!"

My big mouth had just caused a major crisis in my school and personal life. Before the week was out, my friends and I were signed up to join 20,000 competitors on the start line of the Great North Run, in just a few short months.

How was I even going to get past the start line? It takes about ten minutes of running to get to that point when 20,000 people set off.

What was I thinking, running over 13 miles? I was never going to do it. The shame of having to admit that to the super sporty heroes. But what could I do?

I just did it.

I'll always remember the feeling of hitting the home straight, having run 13 miles from city to coast, and feeling the breeze of the cool North Sea against my skin. The roar of the spectators lifted my spirits and injected much needed energy into my tired legs. I'd pounded the roads of the North-East for almost two hours, carried along by the fantastic crowds who turned up in their thousands to cheer us along.

Moments after crossing the finish line to great applause, with a medal around my neck, I bumped into the sporting heroes who'd finished 20 minutes before me. They didn't pat me on the back or praise me, but a certain look, a particular nod and a wink meant I was OK. I'd said I could do it, and I had.

It wasn't long before my two friends crossed the finish to join me, their faces beaming with justified pride in their achievement. Just a few months' previous, we couldn't run around a field. Yet, here we were in South Shields having run 13.1 miles.

How did we do it? When everyone said it was impossible we refused to accept that. We *believed* that we could train to do it.

A training programme in our local newspaper, *The Evening Gazette*, helped us to *relax* and let it happen, to let go of those doubts as a ten minute run became a 15 minute run, then a 30 minute run, then a 45 minute run, and so on.

We relaxed as the distances increased and as we got fitter and fitter. Our breathing got easier, from panting and breathing hard, to breaking that pain barrier and breathing slow, deep and controlled. We started to visualize ourselves as runners, rather than unfit kids doing cross-country. We saved up for decent running shoes and bought running vests. We imagined ourselves crossing that finish line by the sea in South Shields.

Choosing a worthy goal. Belief. Relaxation. Deep Breathing. Success.

Under the Wing of Wisdom

"Your food is ready, if you are?" said Pierce, only a foot or so from my bed.

I jumped clear of the bed with fright.

"Pierce! For goodness sake, you frightened me half to death!" I exclaimed. "I didn't hear you come in."

"Sorry if I startled you. I did knock, and the door was ajar. I was not sure if you were sleeping, or just resting your eyes."

A knock on the door, and the same temple worker who showed me to my room was peering through the half open door. "Your supper is ready, sir, if you would like to follow me?"

I turned to Pierce to check he was coming to eat as well. "I shall wait here a while, if that is all right?" he said. "I wanted to chat to you before we sleep this evening."

"Of course," I said, and followed the man in orange through the temple buildings.

The dining room was less of a room and more of a hall this time, with a lot more temple people munching away at their food in complete silence. A simple dish of fish and rice, washed down with a fruit juice and a small coconut and honey pudding—it was a meal fit for a king, and it made me feel fantastic after a hard day's walking.

On returning to my room, I was surprised to find my guide lying on the bed.

I felt awkward. He'd got a little too close to my comfort zone, in my room, relaxing on my bed, with no sign of shifting.

"The reason I am sitting on your bed, is because I do not want you to lie here at this exact moment. I do not sit here to be rude. Please forgive me."

"I'm not sure what you…"

"I would like you to try one more exercise, as you did today by the river," he said. "If I asked you to do such an exercise lying on your bed, you would likely fall into a restful sleep. We do not want that. We want to be in that special place between waking and sleep, right before you drift into a dream state. Would you be willing to give that a try for me?"

"Of course," I replied. "I'm tired though, so might fall asleep."

"Not whilst sitting on the floor, I fear, for surely you would wake as your head hit the ground."

"Quite," I replied, searching for a smile in the wise man's eyes.

He threw me the pillow from the bed and asked me to get comfortable. It was important to him that I sit upright with my spine erect, in a position that was comfortable to me.

I found it uncomfortable to sit cross-legged on the pillow, so sat in a kneeling position that I'd become used to during my years of judo. My backside rested on my heels as I knelt, my hands on my thighs, spine upright.

He asked me to turn my hands face up, which felt unnatural, but I did as he advised, and awaited further instruction.

"Do you recall the breathing we spoke of during our walk today, that slow, deliberate breathing from the pit of your stomach?"

"Yes."

"Let us begin to breathe together, you and I, in through our noses, and slowly out through our mouths. On the in breath, you may like to gently place your tongue on the roof of your mouth, while on the out breath, relax your tongue and let the breath exhale over it and out into the world."

We began to do this, breathing in for a count of four, and breathing out for a count of eight. On the out breaths he would make a noise, a kind of breathy 'harrrrrrrr' sound, and as we were alone and I felt comfortable, I began to copy him.

In through the nose, out through the mouth.

Within just a few short minutes, I was very, very relaxed. My body became slightly heavy, I could feel the weight of it on the pillow. I'd become aware of my body, yet it was almost as if my body had gone to sleep, and my mind had stayed awake.

After the minutes of breathing, Pierce began to speak to me in a quiet, velvety voice.

He described a journey to me, and asked me to just imagine the things he spoke of. He mentioned a wood, a clearing in the forest, and he suggested I feel the sun on my face and the breeze in my hair.

He spoke of many things, and it felt terrific.

"Three... two... one. Wide awake. Wide awake," he said. "Now, how do you feel?"

"I feel great. Thanks, Pierce. Did I nod off? I feel like I've..."

"No, you did not sleep. Unless you can slumber whilst sitting as straight as an arrow?"

I was still kneeling on the ground on the pillow, my hands palm upwards on my legs. I stood slowly, and did a huge stretch.

"You did very well," he said. "How real was the forest to you?"

I admitted that it felt real enough once I got into it, but that my mind wandered a few times, and sometimes I wasn't sure how to imagine the wood, so I would change aspects and find it distracting. For example, when I pictured the forest, I imagined a canopy of trees where sunlight could not penetrate, a kind of spooky woodland. Yet when he mentioned feeling the rays of sunshine on my face, I had to change the day to a sunny one, and make the trees less dense and further apart.

"This is normal," he said. "You are learning now to let those distracting thoughts drift on by like the clouds on a lazy summer afternoon, as you lie on your back with a piece of grass in your mouth. With practice, with repetition, you will become very good at visualizing while meditating."

"Do you think I was meditating for a moment there, Pierce?" I smiled.

"My friend, you were meditating from the moment you closed your eyes and focussed on your breathing."

"Thank you," I replied. "Thanks." I felt a little emotional, and wasn't sure why.

"Rest now. Perhaps tomorrow we shall see what we can do to bring those imaginings of yours from soft focus to knife-sharp focus."

"I'd like that."

"Oh, and one last thing," he said as he rose and made for the door. "We hit snow tomorrow, so get some sleep and prepare to wrap up warm. You are in for a real treat."

Anything Is Possible

I found the meditation that night astounding. I'd tried meditation many years before after reading a book about 'remote viewing' during the Cold War. Unfortunately, it involved a breathing technique that required covering one nostril while breathing in, then blocking the opposite nostril to breathe out. The technique is well known, but it seemed that every time I tried it, I had a slightly blocked nostril!

Very frustrating, and so I gave up. That night, at the second temple with Pierce, my whole idea of what meditation was simply changed. It became about being very relaxed, just chilling out in a comfy position, and concentrating on my breathing.

I've used the technique many times since my return, and it's so simple that I'd very much like to share it with you now.

First, let's look at our journey so far. In the last chapter, you looked at the need to have faith, to believe, and at the end of that session, you set worthy goals. You're now aware of the need to concentrate on what you *really* want and to write that down in a specific, detailed way.

Now we're looking at the importance of relaxation and the need to be able to sit quietly each day, even if only for a few minutes. What you'll discover very soon is that by thinking of those worthy goals while in that meditative state, you can cause the thing you think about to be created.

I know to some that might sound like science fiction, and yet I know this to be true. I have shared this knowledge with many others before writing this book, and it has been proven true by these people also.

For now, please accept that the starting point in changing your life is to write out on paper what you really want in each key area of your future. You did that the other day; your world is already changing, even though you can't yet see the treasures that are coming your way.

The next step is to learn to quieten your mind, for it is in this relaxed state of meditation that you will consider the goals you've written. You will go over your 'wish list' in this special place, and without any further effort, leave those desires planted deeply in your subconscious mind.

As you'll soon discover, seeds planted in the mind's garden quickly become fruit-bearing trees in the outside world. Anything is possible!

Here then, is a simple example of a meditation I still use today.

YOU ARE FEELING SLEEPY

Switch off your mobile phone (or switch it to silent mode), unplug the landline, stick a 'do not disturb' sign on the front door.

Have a drink of water, make sure you've eaten already; you don't want to be thinking of what you're going to make for lunch while meditating. Not only is it distracting, but it starts your stomach rumbling and can spoil the session.

Choose a place that you'd like to use each time for meditating. Best to avoid your bed if at all possible, as this is associated with sleep, and it's easy to fall asleep (I speak from experience).

Once you have the place, get comfortable. Whatever works best for you—sitting in a normal chair with your spine erect and both feet flat on the floor is fine.

If you're wearing anything restrictive, loosen those items or remove them. I tend to remove my watch and place it on a nearby table so I can still see the time, and I loosen my belt if I'm wearing one.

It will be impossible for you to meditate while reading this page, so please read through the procedure a few times and then give it a go yourself.

Close your eyes, and begin to breathe in through your nose, and out through your mouth.

Breathe in for a count of four or five, and breathe out for a count of eight or ten. Just relax and slowly count in your mind as you begin to bring your attention to your breathing.

Quickly inhale through the nose, and then slowly and deliberately exhale through your mouth. It doesn't matter if you can only breathe in for a count of two and out for a count of four; just try to make the out breath much slower than the in breath, about twice as long if you can.

If I'm alone in my house, I make an audible 'harrrrr' sound as I breathe out. If anyone is in the house, even a few rooms away, I just do the 'harrrr' sound in my head. I'd feel silly if someone asked me why I was making that strange noise!

In breaths, out breaths. Try not to think of anything as you're doing this, just the breaths—in, out, in, out.

If a thought crops up (*"Did I send that email or is it in my drafts folder?"*) ignore it and watch the thought drift across the screen of your mind and away into the distance.

If you need a 'backdrop', imagine a white candle burning against a dark sky, and look only at the flame. Or imagine the sun touching the horizon as it sets or rises; just concentrate on the sun, that orange circle on the black background.

Occasionally, if it's a bad thought, or an all-consuming task that you forgot to do that day, quickly (in your mind) squash the thought bubble into a tight ball, and kick it so hard that it flies out to the horizon like a football kicked off the pitch and into the crowd.

As soon as you feel relaxed, whilst maintaining the slow deep breaths, imagine yourself at the top of a cliff on a hot sunny day.

The cliff in my mind is a real one I enjoyed out in Barbados, a cliff that led to a deserted beach. In my mind over the years, I have manipulated the image or the memory in various ways. One of these ways was to add exactly ten steps down from the low cliff to the sand on the beach. So although I'm on a cliff, it's not a very high one, just ten deep steps down to the beach.

My first five steps curve to the right as they descend, the last five curve to the left. The result is that I don't actually see the beach until the last five steps.

I stand on the cliff, and say out loud (in my head), *"I am going down now, going down to my special place."*

I then count backwards with each step, the first one is ten. Going down to the beach, to that special place.

Nine. Down. Eight, down to the beach. Seven, six, five, I notice the beach, four, I notice the log that acts as a seat on the beach, three, two, I hear the crash of waves, one, I reach out my naked foot and zero, feel the soft, hot white sand between my toes.

I make my way over to the log that has been stripped of its bark and bleached in the Caribbean sun. It's a log I know well, having sat on it many times in my mind's eye. There I sit, looking out to sea, with the cooling breeze rolling in from the breaking waves.

If you're new to meditating, this might all sound very odd. All I can say is that when you dream, it's all very real, isn't it? We see in dreams, we touch, we feel textures, we hear and we smell. With practice, it's possible to do all of these things, whilst meditating.

So when I tell you that I sit on a bleached tree trunk looking out to sea, I mean that it's become quite real. I can often feel the hot wood under my backside, and feel the heat of the sun on my face. I can hear the waves and smell the ozone, almost taste the salt air. I breathe in for five and out for ten, and I'm no longer in my study or summerhouse; I'm breathing in the Caribbean air and smiling with satisfaction, as if I were really there.

To leave the meditation, head back to the steps where you came in, and this time, looking up the steps, start with ten at the bottom.

Leaving the beach, nine, winding to the left a little as you get closer to the top, eight, seven, six, five, winding to the right now as the sound of crashing waves diminish, four, three, two, the top of the cliff is in sight, one, you're at the top, and can start to sense the room around you, and become aware of your body. Wiggle your fingers and toes, and have a good stretch as you open your eyes, wide awake.

All that remains for you to do now is to take action. Just ten minutes a day would do wonders.

Try setting your alarm clock 15 minutes early, and making your way to your quiet place after your morning drink.

Why not put this book down for a moment, and take 15 minutes off your morning alarm clock? Many of us think nothing of staying up for an extra 15 minutes at night to watch the end of a film or TV show. Yet many recoil in horror at the very thought of changing their alarm clock from 7 a.m. to 6.45 a.m.!

Why not change the alarm clock right now, and then come back to this book to finish the chapter?

Please don't just read this book to get an 'overview' and come back to the actions later. Take action now; take action over the next few days as you read this book.

When you rise tomorrow, when you've put the kettle on and woken up, you'll feel great. You'll be pleased with yourself for taking action. Then spend ten minutes in a quiet place with your eyes closed.

You've identified what you want in life, you've done some meditation, and in the next chapter you'll learn how to combine these two aspects to create the life of your dreams.

If your list of desires were a firework, and basic meditation the fuse, then the knowledge Pierce shared with me on Day Three would be the lit match.

CHAPTER THREE

*"Visualize this thing that you want, see it, feel it,
believe in it. Make your mental blueprint,
and begin to build."*
— **ROBERT COLLIER** *(1885–1950)*

Visualize

It all started much earlier than expected, when I awoke in a smoke-filled room with someone yelling, *"Fire! Fire!"*

I leapt to my feet and planted my head into a layer of thick grey smoke.

The room was still fairly dark—no fire in there—but I could see the silhouette of Pierce against the open door, lit from behind by a flickering orange glow.

As I began to cough, he spoke to me in his usual slow, relaxing manner, as if everything around him were completely normal.

"For a moment, I thought I had been working you too hard up this little mountain. I had to shout 'Fire' several times before you woke."

He seemed completely unaffected by the smoke. I couldn't stop coughing and instinctively lowered my head closer to the floor, covering my mouth with my bandana.

A small fire had broken out in the cooking area just minutes before Pierce had burst in and awakened me from deep sleep. We quickly assembled our things as the temple occupants worked to put out the fire.

By the time we stuffed fruit into our backpacks and headed for the main doors, the flames were out and people were already starting to laugh in whispers as they tidied the aftermath.

"Our friends will be short of water today. We shall fill our drink bottles in a little while," said Pierce.

With bleary eyes and the taste of smoke in my mouth, I set off into the near darkness.

Hitting the Trail

The sun was only just beginning to yawn over the horizon of jet-black mountain peaks. The ground began to sparkle, the frozen earth reflecting the rays like a carpet of scattered diamonds.

"It feels wonderful, does it not, to rise so early and admire the mountain trail?" said Pierce.

"Yes!" I replied, already struggling for breath as the cold morning air chilled my throat. "It does."

I tried not to think about the fact that I had blisters, stiff aching legs and a sore back, not to mention the recurring breathlessness. I chose instead to look on the bright side: at least the terrible headache I had at the start had gone, and aside from the retching caused by smoke inhalation that morning, I was no longer coughing.

After an hour of ascending a difficult rock-strewn path scattered with ice, we began to descend into a remote steep-sided ravine. From a distance, the sides of the valley looked smooth, as if created by a giant axe hitting soft clay. The descent was slow, snaking in one direction for ten minutes, then the opposite direction for a further ten minutes, then back the other way.

My knees began to ache with the downward jolting of the deep rocky steps. Pierce lengthened his stride and moved ahead. By this point I was more than happy to let him do so, and made no effort to keep up. I wanted to make it to the summit, and had to pace myself to preserve my knee and ankle joints. I also tried to stretch my legs and back whenever possible to ease the pain.

Pierce had walked ahead to check a natural spring. I found him sitting within easy reach of the pure mountain water, sheltered from the cold morning breeze yet illuminated by the rising sun. The spring had frozen at different layers, creating a brilliant white pipe to fill our bottles from—ice cold purified mountain water on demand. I sat down and pulled some fruit from my rucksack.

"How are your legs holding up today?" Pierce asked.

"A little stiff," I replied, trying to sound positive, "but still working."

"Perhaps you could imagine, in your mind's eye, what it would be like to have strong healthy legs?" He reached out to touch his toes with ease. "Could you visualize your leg muscles repairing themselves at speed? The fibres replenished and strengthened for the day ahead?"

"I guess so," I replied. "Although to be honest, I'd find it hard to visualize healthy legs while they hurt so much."

"And yet, in that place of deep relaxation we spoke of just yesterday, there is no leg pain, only possibility."

"Yes, I suppose so."

"The key to the door of untold happiness is visualization, my friend. Without it, we are a ship without sails, tossed around upon the oceans created by others. We need to consider what we *really* want in our lives, what *really* brings happiness, then we need to commit those to paper. You have started to do that already.

"When we write them down, we think about what it would be like to have, be, or do those things, right? My advice is to work hard to intensify those visualizations.

"Imagine you want to visit the pyramids of Egypt. Let us be very specific. Imagine you want to arrive at the Giza Plateau in Cairo, at sunrise, on a camel."

Pierce smiled as he unscrewed his old water bottle.

"Rather than picture a vague fuzzy image of what that might be like, we must imagine what that would *feel* like. Perhaps the desert air is cold against your face, you are holding on tight trying to get used to the rhythm of the camel rocking back and forth. Maybe the camel smells like, like a camel."

Pierce grinned and then took a small sip of water.

"Other smells might fill your nostrils—the scent of flowers, the smell of cooking, of herbs and spices, of nearby camp fires. Imagine the sounds, the noise of the early morning Cairo suburbs. Cars and motorcycles sounding their horns, radios playing at the side of the streets where people gather around fires, perhaps smoking their shisha pipes.

"As the camel slowly plods onto the cold sands of the Giza Plateau, the noise lessens, replaced by the rhythmic jangle of the camel's reins. Picture the first sight of the Great Pyramid itself, hundreds of feet of ancient mystery and wonder. What would that look like?"

I smiled knowingly. "Yes Pierce, I remember it well."

Had I told him I'd travelled over the desert sands to the pyramids of Giza at sunrise? Had I mentioned I did it on camel back? I couldn't remember.

"It matters not whether you have been there already or are planning to go there for the first time. What matters is that you can visualize the whole experience *as if* it is happening right now, this very minute. Not just the sights, but the sounds, the smells, the tastes, the *feel* of the whole experience."

At this point, the ugly hand of doubt ran its spindly fingers through my hair, as I began to question my ability to visualize so vividly.

"What if I close my eyes, Pierce, and just see swirls of colours on the back of my eyelids? What if I can't see these things?"

Pierce smiled, and stretched his neck, moving his left ear towards his left shoulder, and then his right ear to his right shoulder.

"Your mind acts like a muscle, my friend. Look at your biceps, and imagine that I place your left arm in a sling for a month or two. Then I ask you to lift a dumbbell every other day with your right arm. At the end of the two months, when you remove the sling from your left arm, your right bicep will be much bigger than the left, which will have become smaller.

78

"Do absolutely nothing with your mind, and it will be like an untrained muscle. It still works its wonders, but at a tiny fraction of its potential. Train it regularly, even ten minutes per day, and it will become a force to be reckoned with. It can become a finely tuned instrument of pure creation.

"The person who meditates early in the morning, last thing at night, and even at midday for a few minutes, is in a position to experience heaven on Earth."

"So you're saying that if I can't see vivid pictures when I close my eyes, I should just practice? Maybe I'm just impatient, Pierce, but if I still couldn't see anything after a few days, I just know I'd start feeling like I couldn't do it."

"Indeed, and if you *feel* you cannot do it, this will become your reality. Things will happen to distract you, to prevent you from practising each morning, to keep your mind on other matters. You will fulfil your own prophecy, and not be able to meditate.

"You *can* meditate. You do so already when you daydream. When your mind wanders and you imagine your next holiday, only to snap out of it and remember you are driving on a main road and your junction is coming up, that is a form of meditation.

"Any obstacles you choose to create are just that—obstacles you put in the way. Do not consider for a moment why this is not for you, because this is the way to true happiness and the life waiting for you."

"I guess you're right."

"I am indeed correct," Pierce smiled. "Have you heard the little story about the man who dies and is met by angels?"

"I'm not sure, which one?"

"A man dies and is greeted by two angels. One angel has a broad, happy smile; the other angel wears a smile that hides sadness. Each angel takes one of the man's hands and they ascend towards the light, which grows brighter and brighter. The light dims, and the man finds himself standing before two doors.

"The angel on the man's right, wearing the broad smile, unlocks the door to the right. Through the open door, the man sees paradise.

"'Come,' says the angel, 'for you have led a wonderful life on Earth and now it is time to relax in a warm, bountiful afterlife, for all eternity.'

"The man sees rolling green hills lit by a beautiful soft sun, a lake filled by a spectacular waterfall. Snow-capped mountains sit on the horizon, while the scents of the nearby flowers fill the air with perfume and butterflies dance on the warm breeze. 'Thank you,' says the man. 'I am truly blessed.' He pauses before stepping through the doorway. 'What is behind the door to the left?'

"'Oh,' replies the other angel, his forced smile disappearing to reveal sadness. 'You do not want to see in there, for it is a dreadful place.'

"The man shudders. 'Is it… hell?'

"'You might say that, but not in the way you were told during your life. It is far worse.'

"'Can I take a look? Just a peek before I go through the door to paradise?'

"The angel lowers his gaze to the floor in sadness, and unlocks the door. The man gazes inside, confused. The scene looks familiar. 'Why, this is my old house, the one we had to sell when times got tough! I loved this house! The one after this was tiny and damp, but this one was great.'

"The man walks around the house, admiring it. 'Something is wrong here. It's too perfect.' He sees the garden he always wanted to create, a hot tub and pool, the new double garage he never built, and in it, the car of his dreams. The man walks reluctantly back towards the angels, with a look of confusion on his face. This place was a million times better than the place through the other door. It was everything he loved and desired, much more.

"'You told me this was like hell, but it was filled with the best of everything, a perfect life. Why did you try to stop me taking a look in there?'

"The sad angel closes the door. 'My dearest child. That is the life you were destined to live on Earth, if only you had believed. It was the life you were born to live, but didn't.'"

Pierce held a fixed serious stare at me as he finished the little story, before smiling and rising.

"You are meant to live a full, happy and bountiful life, full of wonder and awe. *You* were born to live a rich, abundant life. Come," he continued. "Let us live like great kings, that do wondrous things for the people of our kingdom."

With that, he adjusted the straps of his haversack and left the shelter of the spring at a pace. The rest stop was over.

A Peak Ahead

It took some time to catch up to Pierce, as he dug in hard with his staff and ascended the rocky steps. Boulders and rocks bunched up together on the steep slope, providing stone steps at knee height to challenge even the strongest thighs.

I finally caught up to him.

"Let us ponder the things we have spoken of," he said, through lightly clenched teeth. "We can talk more at the top of this rise."

He dodged loose stones, jumped from one rock to another, then ducked and weaved up the mountain like a sprightly boxer.

The sight at the top of the next rise lifted my heart—a snow-covered peak. Pierce smiled at my wide eyes. "We shall be walking in snow by this afternoon, and stay that way until we summit."

"Will we get to that peak today?" I asked, hoping it would be saved for fresher legs the next day.

"No, we shall skirt around that particular peak and descend into camp by nightfall. Tomorrow, if we rise early enough, we will get our first glimpse of the top."

We began the gentle descent into a valley and my legs relaxed. "I'm looking forward to practising this 'visualization' tonight," I told

Pierce. "I'm going to try and recall the sights and sounds of my trip to the pyramids, like you said."

"Let me suggest a simpler visualization to ease you into using your senses in meditation. When you are rested this evening, and alone in your room, close your eyes and breathe for a while as I have shown you.

"Picture in your mind's eye a place that you know very well. It could be a favourite room in your home, or the front door to your house. Choose a place where you do not have to 'strain' to remember, a place already etched into the fabric of your mind.

"Let us imagine you chose the front door to your home. You might begin with the sense of sight. What colour is the door? Is the door handle to the left or to the right? What does the door handle look like? Is there glass in the door? If so, is it plain, or stained glass, rippled or smooth? Does it have a number on the door itself? If it does, what colour is the number? What shape? Is it proud of the door or flat against it like a sticker? Look very closely, my friend.

"Next, while standing close to the door, you might introduce the sense of touch. If the image of your front door is still fuzzy, reach out to the softly focussed surface and touch it. Rub the front door, and you could well find it taking form, becoming more real in your mind. Is it hot to the touch, perhaps heated by the midday sun? Or is it cold, maybe a man-made material, chilled by the winter frost? Is the door smooth or rough? Is there glass in the door? If so, does the paintwork feel different from the glass? Does the keyhole have sharp edges? Is there a door knocker you can touch or move around?

"Now, listen carefully to the sounds around you. Do you hear the chorus of birdsong, or the sound of wind rustling through trees? Perhaps you hear the sound of children playing in the nearby school or park, maybe the background noise of traffic, or the distant hum of the main road.

"All of the senses can be used, so we might introduce the sense of smell, perhaps even taste. That may sound too far, but worry not, for nobody is watching when we do this in our mind!" He laughed out loud, pausing for a moment with his right foot perched atop a high rock.

"What if you had chosen to imagine your kitchen, rather than your front or back door? Using smell would be easy: you could smell the herbs on the window sill, the bananas in the fruit bowl, or the food in the pantry. You could taste the fruit juice in the fridge by licking the top of the carton!

"Do not just see the image. For some the image is fuzzy or blurred, but touch the image, smell it, listen to it, and if you can, taste it. Each of these senses provides an opportunity to greatly intensify your ability to visualize clearly in your mind.

"Once you have practised this, you have enhanced the ability to create an image in your mind and are close to being able to imagine how the situation would *feel* in your heart."

A Sense of Awareness

"We are taught in school that we have only five senses: sight, sound, touch, taste and hearing. Occasionally we hear of a mystical 'sixth sense', which indeed we all have, although it lies largely dormant in most. The truth is that we have dozens of senses."

Pierce pushed down on his left leg and thrust himself up onto the rock, so he was standing on one foot, his arms flaying around like the wings of a fledgling bird.

"What about your sense of balance? Is that not a sense? We have a sense of balance, do we not?"

"Well, I guess so. I never thought of it quite like that. I…"

He stopped balancing and stood firm with both feet on the rock.

"What about heat?" he continued. "We worked up quite a sweat climbing earlier. Did we not *feel* hot? That was not our sense of touch, was it? What if we lie in the sun with our eyes closed, and sense the sun's heat on our faces? Is that a sense of heat, perhaps?"

I found these ideas baffling. Pierce jumped down from the boulder, and began to amble downhill, looking over his shoulder to check I was following.

"What about the sense of hunger we are both feeling right now? Or the sense of thirst we would feel if our water were to run out? Surely these are senses? How are your blisters, by the way?"

"Oh, I've got blisters on blisters," I joked. "But they're numb at the moment. I feel those more when we stop and rest for a while."

"When you sense the pain of your blisters, or your throbbing thighs, or your aching back – are you not using another sense? The sense of pain, perhaps?

"You have dozens of senses, my friend, but I look upon these as 'sub-senses'. For the purpose of manifesting the life of your dreams, I look upon the multitude of overlooked senses as one single seventh sense: *the sense of awareness.*

"Aristotle had his five senses. We all have an intuitive sixth sense if we choose to use it, and I take immense pleasure in introducing you to your seventh sense, for all human beings have this innate sense of awareness.

If you *feel* something, then this is the seventh sense, be it hunger, thirst, heat, cold, or sympathy, empathy. Excitement? Surely we can have a sense of excitement. Not forgetting the most important of all of these senses that fall within the Sense of Awareness – a sense of Gratitude. Powerful and essential, we could perhaps discuss that when we have more time. Look, we are almost at the valley floor."

My brain ached at the notion of having seven senses, and yet I agreed with the numerous sub-senses that Pierce had assembled under his 'seventh sense' banner.

I finally spoke up as Pierce turned sharply to lead us up the steep bank out of the valley. "If the sixth sense is dormant, I suppose we should not only use the five senses we're familiar with in our visualizations, but also this seventh sense as well?"

Pierce stopped dead in his tracks. "Shukriya! Thank you. Your assumption is correct."

A broad smile erupted over his weathered face.

"When we calm our minds and are ready to create our future, we see it as if it is already here. We then touch it in our mind, we smell it, taste it, and hear it—exactly how it will be when it is really in your life, every detail.

"However, the most crucial sense to use is the sense of awareness—how will this thing in your future make you *feel*?"

He looked up the mountain, and then turned to beckon me to his side. We began the slow ascent.

"Consider a lazy summer evening. You are relaxing with friends. The sun is low in the sky amidst dazzling swirls of purple, red and orange. The scent of freshly mown grass and flowers fills the air, then the smell of hot food cooking on the barbeque. You hear the chatter of friends and the clinking of glasses.

"You close your eyes, and notice a cool breeze brush your sun-kissed cheeks. You lift your glass to your lips and feel the ice cold drink travel down your throat.

"How do you feel? How would you feel in that situation?

"You might smile as you look at the sunset with your drink in your hand, cuddle your loved ones, soak up the atmosphere and feel really content.

"Did you know you can feel that exact sense of well-being during your time of relaxation? I do so daily.

"Now, let us imagine a scenario that has yet to come. How would we use the method I describe?

"Let us imagine that you desire an attractive partner who makes you laugh. Relaxed in your meditation, you would begin to picture this lucky person."

Pierce smiled, and looked skyward. His pause seemed to indicate a recollection from a long time ago.

"Your mind may wander to a situation where you might see this perfect partner. Perhaps you visualize them jogging on the beach or walking a dog in the park. It matters not; just try to form an image of this perfect partner in your mind.

"As we mentioned their ability to induce laughter in you, then perhaps we would smile in the meditation, maybe laugh out loud with them. This smile could break through from the imagined world to the real world, causing you to grin while you meditate in your quiet place. I often do this, I love to smile with gratitude whilst meditating.

"The key here is to *feel* as if it is happening for real. Next, bring in the other senses. How do they sound? Do they talk in a high voice or a soft husky voice? Do they have the same accent as you, or are they from out of town, or even from overseas? Is their speech fast and excited, or slow and deliberate?

"You are in the act of creation. What do you really want? Tall or small, black or white, well-built or slim, blonde or brunette, and all the other combinations out there.

"Use your sense of smell next. As you hug in your mind, what perfume or cologne do they wear? Does their hair smell of shampoo? Let your imagination soar.

"Run your fingers through their hair; how does that feel? As you stroke the person's cheek with a feather-light touch, what does their skin feel like?

"Finally, the seventh sense. How does this beautiful person make you feel? You may feel love in your heart, but also a sense of deep connection, perhaps they are your soul mate. Or you may feel aroused, yet also feel great contentment.

"Think about how you feel during the meditation. Really think about how this perfect partner makes you feel.

"Exercising our imagination one last time, wrap the whole experience in a bubble of gratitude. Just imagine a ball of light forming around the whole scene and watch it take off on the breeze like a helium balloon. As it floats high in the sky, you know that your very specific desire is soaring into the Universe, and will surely come to pass in the real world.

"By the time you complete the meditation, you feel marvellous, and you feel terrific all day."

The Twinkling Village

By the time we crossed the snow line several hours later, my mind was ablaze with possibility.

Pierce had shared numerous scenarios for me in my mind, and although the climbing had been tough on my legs and back, I had become largely unaware of any discomfort.

Instead, as Pierce talked, I'd once again journeyed home in my mind to certain rooms in my house. I'd also relaxed in a summer meadow, and sat in a rocking chair at night to watch the stars. He even had me imagining what it would be like to soar like a bird on the breeze, over the treetops and down over a deep blue lake.

It was great fun, and showed me that if we let ourselves go, there are no limits at all to what we might imagine.

"How are you faring in this snow?" Pierce asked, interrupting my thoughts.

"Oh, er, fine," I replied, having not realized the snow was deeper now, at a level just below the knee.

"We are losing the light fast, my friend. Perhaps you should ready your head torch."

"Thanks," I said, pulling the light from a side pocket. "Do you have one yourself?"

Pierce chuckled. "No, no. I prefer my night vision."

I switched the head torch to red, so as not to ruin Pierce's night vision, and made a mental note to eat more carrots.

As we finally reached the top of the snowy ridge, darkness was upon us. The moon was almost full, guiding us along the icy trail. As

I caught sight of the twinkling lanterns of a village in the valley just a few hundred feet below, Pierce spoke to me in his usual hushed tones.

"I hope what I have shared with you today has been useful?"

"Absolutely. I'm going to try to visualize again tonight, before I fall asleep."

"I am pleased to hear that," he said. "I have one more exercise for you to consider, before you sleep tonight if you are not too tired? For now, let us locate the temple."

With that, he began to bound downhill in the deep snow, barely visible in the light of my head torch.

"OK Pierce, wait up!" I said as I too lifted my feet high out of the knee-deep snow and began to leap in exaggerated strides down the hill.

I didn't have time to register the fact that he'd found another temple for us to stay in, nor to bask in the relief of having a warm meal and a roof over my head. He was off, at a rate of knots, towards the twinkling lights of the village below.

The snow was deep enough to soak up the impact of each significant stride as we descended at great speed. We slid occasionally, jumped perhaps six feet sometimes from one section to another, and never slowed the pace.

It was invigorating and at the same time terrifying. I placed my life in the hands of my wise mountain guide, for all I could do in the moonlight was follow the shape of Pierce as he darted towards the village like a downhill slalom skier.

Lanterns and Torches

At the bottom of the hill we stopped to gather our thoughts and catch our breath. Ahead stood a magical village, lit by lanterns and the flicker of torches and small fires.

Pierce inhaled deeply through his nose and breathed out through his mouth slowly. "Ready?" he said with that large, friendly smile that wrinkled his eyes. "Come, let us eat and recuperate."

The lanterns swayed and the torches flickered, casting eerie shadows on the whitewashed walls, which glowed as yellow as the flames that lit them.

The buildings were sturdier than the previous villages, and more ornate. Most of the windows had shutters, and some of the roofs were curved and built more solidly. I reasoned that they were built that way to cope with the amount of snowfall.

An elderly lady appeared at the door to her home and emptied a pot of dirty water into a makeshift channel that ran down the street. She spoke out a greeting in the local tongue that felt like, "Good evening."

Most people were in their houses or murmuring around communal fires in front of their homes. Occasionally someone would look up, nod their head to acknowledge us, and then shout something to a neighbour. A conversation would then break out between the neighbours, which lessened in volume as we continued to walk in the direction of the temple.

"We have no crowds gathering today, Pierce," I said with a smile, checking behind me into the darkness.

"Indeed. The people of this village are good folk, although I find they do tend to worry about all manner of things."

"Worry?"

"Yes, they doubt themselves, and worry about food supplies, the weather, the dry season, the wet season." Pierce laughed. "Everything really."

"I see."

"I have seen a few squabbles here over the years. The locals seem quick to blame others for their perceived misfortune, rather than taking a long, hard look at themselves. Ultimately of course, we are each responsible for our own thoughts and actions, and therefore fully responsible for the world we have created for ourselves."

Pierce stopped next to a blazing torch, his white beard flashing yellow in time with the crackles and hisses.

"Here," he said. "Take the torch, we shall return it tomorrow."

Leaving the main street, we began to ascend a small hill where a large temple came into view in the moonlight.

As I drew closer, torch in hand, the whole whitewashed exterior lit up like some giant yellow lantern. Three arches decorated the rather ornate entrance, with various symbols carved into the wood.

Before I could locate a door knocker or bell, the large door began to open inwards. With a loud creak and a groan, amplified by the quiet of the night, the door opened to reveal a frail-looking old man wearing little round spectacles.

He reached out with a toothless smile, and took the flambeau from me, placing his other hand around my back to escort me in.

Pierce nodded, smiled, and followed in silence, as a second temple occupant appeared from the shadows to quietly close the door.

We'd made it safely to the sanctuary of another temple.

Moments later, in my small room, I recorded in my diary how happy I was with the routine that was unfolding.

Pierce was choosing a route up the mountain that allowed us several stops in temples on the way. We had shelter from the elements, a bed, and warm food. I felt so content.

I was also quickly getting used to the idea of a 'catnap' before supper.

Back home I would resist this urge for fear of it affecting my ability to sleep later that night. Yet here, after a hard day's walking, I could relax and slowly drift in comfort, easily sleeping after supper. Maybe it was all that fresh air.

I sat up on my low bed to attend to my blisters. Not just a straw filled mattress, but an actual low bed—a firm mattress raised a foot or more off the floor by ornate wooden blocks.

The room was slightly larger than the last, and I'd managed to find a wash bowl as I scanned the room by candlelight.

My blisters were looking a lot better now, and starting to heal. It was great to dress them and put clean socks on as I gently eased myself back onto the bed with a groan.

If only I could rest my leg muscles for a day, and sort out my back-pack to try and ease my lower back pain, I'd be a happy man. I'd still be breathless, but now that my runny nose had gone, along with the coughing and headaches of previous days, I'd be in much better shape.

I stretched and yawned loudly, smiling to myself at the luxury of this simple bed. Then I found myself reflecting on the wise words that my mountain guide had shared that day.

Robin Hood to the Rescue

Now that I pondered the subject, I could see where I had used visualization at key points in my life, without even realizing it. A good example was my Equity Card.

The British Actors' Equity Association is the union that I needed to join if I were to become a professional stuntman. Initially I'd be required to join as an actor or performer. Then, after working for a few years in TV or theatre, I could apply for full membership of the union. Then and only then could I complete my stunt training and apply for membership of the elusive Stunt Register.

At the age of 22, I was still at home with my parents. We lived in the northeast, in a small village called Ormesby, positioned on the border of North Yorkshire where I was born. I knew the life I wanted to live, but had no idea of how I was going to get from the life I had, to the life I could barely dream of.

I was trapped in a nine to five job at a local school, in an area without any form of film or television work, and no obvious routes to break into acting. Was my dream of starring in Hollywood movies just that, a dream?

By 22, I'd been training on and off for four years. I had already qualified in judo, fencing, parachuting, swimming, hang-gliding and scuba diving. The training would all be in vain unless I could obtain my Equity

Card, but there was a catch. You had to be an actor or performer in order to get your Equity Card, and in order to get work as an actor or performer, you had to have an Equity Card!

Impossible. Yet, if I were ever going to become a stuntman, I had to somehow gain my union card. I would have to become a paid performer.

| "Who Goes There?" |

Four months later, I stood with my knees knocking, in the shadows of The Sheriffs Lodge, Nottingham.

I was lurking in the dark to hide from an expectant medieval banquet audience, who awaited the hero of the hour.

My knees were knocking because I was that hero—Robin Hood!

Dressed in Sherwood green from head to toe, with a sword in my belt and my heart in my mouth, I awaited my cue atop a high balcony to the left of the banqueting hall's performing area. Below I could see the actor playing Sir Guy of Gisborne grab Maid Marion and drag her centre stage; my entrance was imminent.

When he tried to steal a kiss from the fair maiden, she retorted, "I'd rather kiss the backside of an adder!" This was my cue to stand by.

Sir Guy grabbed her as the minstrel compère teased the audience. "There's nobody to save her now, but wait—who goes there?" My cue!

I stood up, dropped the rope that had been hidden on the balcony, and swung down to land at the feet of Gisborne.

"Hooray! It's Robin Hood!" shouted the compère, as the banqueting hall erupted to cheers and much table bashing.

As the crowd began to chant, "*Robin, Robin, Robin,*" Gisborne swung at me wildly with his sword. I ducked, allowing him to hit a wooden beam hard enough to send splinters flying. A sword fight ensued that had the audience on their feet, the sparks of the real steel blades spitting molten metal as they clanged and clashed around the hall.

It was brilliant. Especially since I had only found out 30 minutes before curtain call that I was playing the lead role!

Though I didn't know it at the time, it was visualization that got me from being a 'trapped wannabe' to a paid performer, in just a few short months.

| The Visit |

Earlier that year the BBC had broadcast a documentary about a man called Paul Jennings. Paul wanted to become a stuntman, and the documentary, called *The Visit*, followed his progress through his years of training, to his acceptance onto the British Stunt Register. I saw it when I'd already been training to be a stuntman for a while, at a time when the dark curtain of doubt was beginning to descend.

I watched, captivated, slightly envious, as this young man became a professional stuntman.

The climax of the documentary was Paul's first stunt job, for a famous stunt coordinator named Wayne Michaels. Wayne had doubled for Pierce Brosnan as 007 in the famous jump from the Verzasca dam in Switzerland, for the opening sequence of the Bond film *GoldenEye*. (I now know Wayne well, and have since worked for him, and with him, and have been to his house, and had tea and homemade cake with his wife Tracey!}

What was interesting was that Paul got his Equity Card in two ways. He performed in medieval banquets as a jester, and he performed in a live jousting show—the medieval sport of charging on horseback towards your opponent with a heavy lance, hoping to knock them off their steed.

After the documentary, I thought of little else. Medieval banquets. Jousting shows.

What excited me about the banquets and jousting was that I could already use a sword—I was a sword fencing instructor for the local university by this time—and I could also ride.

I didn't realize at the time that the foil I'd become quite adept with bore little resemblance to a heavy broadsword, nor did I appreciate that my ability on a horse was far from the required standard to slip on a suit of armour and charge down the tilt towards a galloping knight!

The Nottingham Jousting Association was, and still is, based in Bunny, Leicestershire. I tracked down the owner of the troop, Sam Humphrey, and asked about getting involved. I was young, keen, could use a sword and ride. Did he need anyone to help out at his shows?

He did. I still recall the excitement of driving to Nottingham Castle, where Sam and his guys were performing at the annual Robin Hood Festival in the castle grounds.

The show was excellent, and Sam was courteous and accommodating. He admired my willingness to travel 120 miles to see the show and meet him, and told me to look him up the moment I moved to Nottingham. My imaginings were becoming real.

Returning to my day job on Monday was difficult. It was a great job at the local school, but I was becoming like a bear trapped in a small enclosure at a run-down zoo. I wanted out.

I immediately began to imagine a move to Nottingham. I also started to plan how and when I might give notice to my employer. I remember pacing up and down my bedroom, looking at the brochure for the Robin Hood Festival. My heart would flutter, half excitement, half nerves, at the experiences the jousting troop might provide.

Although I'd been invited to join the Nottingham Jousting Association, we hadn't discussed money. What if the role of squire was unpaid and only the guys with lines who rode horses got paid?

I needed something else.

As my bedroom pacing wore the carpet bare, I'd glance at an image of a medieval banquet on my cork board. If only I could find a banqueting hall!

| The Lodge |

It was soon after, approaching the Christmas of 1992, that I had a 'lucky break'. A chance encounter with a friend of a friend led to an invitation from the director of a group of performers called Pavanne Promotions. Pavanne supplied actors, performers, dancers and variety artists to a popular medieval banqueting hall in Nottingham.

Lucky break? Chance encounter? From my temple bed I began to realize they were nothing of the sort.

Years of struggle had preceded that decision to find a banquet to perform in, years in which I began to slowly shift my focus from being a stuntman, to "What if I can't make it as a stuntman? What then?"

That vibration sent out a message into the Universe of 'not being a stuntman', a frequency of lack and limitation. That in turn attracted to me people, situations and circumstances that held me back. Lack of finances, injury, a spate of poor weather for parachuting or hang-gliding—I used to think I was cursed.

And then, one day, some tiny spark appeared: the TV documentary, the idea of starring in a medieval banquet. I latched onto that idea, it *felt* right deep inside me.

I thought about it a lot. I imagined what costume I'd wear, I thought about what kind of sword routines I might perform. I visualized fire breathing and fire eating as Paul had done in the TV show; how hard could it be? I imagined the flames billowing from my mouth, the clash of steel blade, the fair maidens and the mead.

Then, the banquet found its way to me. Though I didn't understand it at the time, I attracted it into my life by my sustained thoughts and actions.

So I drove down to meet the director at his home in Barrow upon Soar, Leicestershire. His name was Davey Slater, a friendly man, who introduced me to his wife Karon, his daughter Kelly, and her best friend Rachel, both 15 years old. Then we all climbed into a car and shot off to the banqueting hall, where the 'audition' would take place.

This audition was actually dressing up in a spare medieval surcoat and joining in that evening's performance!

I quickly got changed in the banqueting hall, a former primary school converted into a permanent medieval hall, complete with all the timbers, shields, flags, hardy benches and top table you might expect.

I wore a roomy white shirt and a tight pair of black leggings, which left nothing to the imagination. Luckily, my embarrassment was spared by a long blue surcoat that came down to a little above the knee. A black belt with a shiny buckle held it all together.

No sooner had I finished changing than the show's villain arrived. Neil had a strong Birmingham accent, a hard face and long matted black hair. His dark eyes were shark-like, and he looked the sort you wouldn't want to meet in a dark alley.

Davey introduced me as someone looking to get involved, and mentioned I was a fencing instructor. Neil looked me up and down, nodded in silence, and began to get changed.

Moments later, the cast began to murmur about the actor who played Robin Hood—he was running late. Neil resurfaced with a couple of swords. They were 'foils', not the heavy broadswords that the other actors tucked into their belts.

Neil threw me the sword. "I'm glad we have a fencing coach to show us all what to do, I've done a bit of sword stuff in my time..." He spat and wiped his mouth. "Come on then."

It had all the feel of a playground bully testing the new kid at school. Before I had chance to talk my way out of it, Neil lunged at me with his foil. I instinctively parried his attack, as I had done countless times when teaching the students of Teesside University.

He attacked again and again, few of his vicious blows landing, much to his disgust. I blocked a particularly ferocious attack and automatically reposted to his shoulder with a hard prod—he had no defence. The gathering cast, now joined by the director Davey, took a collective in-breath.

What followed was a frenzied attack, where all rules went out of the window, as he tried to whip me repeatedly like a cane-bearing teacher who had finally snapped. I blocked attack after attack, and when the odd lunge made contact, I'd repost with a dig to the ribs or his solar plexus. This made him more and more angry, and as he lost focus, he lost concentration.

I began to enjoy whipping him back. The rules of foil were not in force; he was actually using his sword like a sabre, which, unbeknown to Neil, was my favourite weapon.

As he began to tire and slow down, I began to show off. After all, I was being tested for a place on the banquet team!

At length Neil backed down with a bloodied hand, admitting "Enough is enough." The bully had been defeated.

He retired to his dressing room to tend to his hand. I acted blasé about the whole episode, but inside I was grinning from ear to ear. It could have easily gone the other way, and I'd have left with my tail between my legs, never to return. But it hadn't—I'd stood up to the playground bully, and was on top of the world.

Moments later, as more and more guests gathered behind the doors, Davey beckoned me over.

"Curtis, er, we have a slight problem that you may be able to help us with. I don't know how to tell you this but..."

I thought I was going to be sacked before I'd begun. Had I taken the sword fighting challenge too seriously? Gone too far?

"We have no Robin," Davey said, interrupting my thoughts. "You want me to play Robin Hood?!"

Davey screwed his face up in discomfort – it was a big ask. "Well, yes. But we'll cover for you, you don't have to learn the lines, and we can cut the fight right down."

"I'd love to."

"And we can work around the script by shouting at Sir Guy, the lines you would normally...hang on...you'd love to?" His face beamed in delight. "Thank you!"

And that, dear reader, is how I ended up dressed in green, with my knees knocking, a sword in my belt and my heart in my mouth, awaiting my cue high in The Sheriff's Lodge.

I went on to become good friends with Neil, learned to fire breathe like Paul Jennings in the documentary, and I even ended up at the same riding school as Paul, with the same instructor as Paul, learning to joust in the same jousting team as Paul!

The Dream Board

Dinner was early that night, brought to my door by a temple worker. Just as well really, as I was extremely tired.

Pierce dropped by a little later. I took great delight in sharing with him my realization that visualization had been the key to me gaining my Equity Card.

"Indeed," replied Pierce in his usual slow, deliberate manner. "Let me ask you something. You say you thought of nothing else. Did you surround yourself with words and pictures of this lofty goal?"

"Yes, I guess I did. I pinned a few brochures on my noticeboard above my desk, which showed people at a banquet, and also one of a jousting contest. And after meeting Sam at Nottingham Castle, I pinned his card and a leaflet from the Robin Hood Pageant to my board as well."

"Interesting," he grinned, running his fingers through his beard. "And do you still do that? Do you still add images to this noticeboard of yours?"

"No, I don't really have a set-up like that at the moment. That was in my old bedroom at my mum and dad's house."

"Might I suggest you start up that practice once again?"

"Why?"

"Because without realizing it, my friend, you had put together a Dream Board.

"On this board, you place photos, drawings, images and words. Words are very important too, as words can create that all-important *feeling* just as much as a photograph can, often more so.

"Hang the board somewhere prominent, where you will glance at it from time to time during the day. Try to make it part of your daily routine to look at your board every morning. Make it one of the first things you do.

"Finally, take another good look before you go to sleep at night. This glance is especially important, for it allows our subconscious mind to work on the challenge while you sleep."

"The challenge?" I asked, fascinated by what I was learning.

"The challenge to move you from where you are now to where you want to be. The challenge to move you from the home you live in now, to the home that is pinned on your vision board."

"I see," I replied. "That's great, although I work away a lot and don't have a desk or anything during the day."

"That is fine," Pierce added with a huge smile. "Then you would create a Vision Book—a Dream Book, a Book of Life—call it what you will. Get yourself a good quality journal-type book that appeals to you, perhaps a hardback book that feels nice to the touch, go for something special; maybe it has a magnetic catch, or even a little lock and key. Choose something that resonates with you.

"Instead of pinning photos, words and statements to your board, you can paste them in your book and write the words and phrases. Then it comes down to opening the book in the morning, glancing at it during the day, and looking at it before you retire for the evening."

"That's perfect," I said with gusto. "I'll do just that. Pierce, I understand the idea of finding photos to match your goals, but what words would I use? I'm not sure I'm clear on that?"

"My advice would be to use two types of words or phrases. One is a single word, two at the most, that sets the scene. For example, love, bliss, luxury, contentment, joy, peace, serenity, abundance, wealth, comfort.

"The other is a phrase, an affirmation of sorts, that states your situation as if the dream were already realized in the physical world. An example might be 'I am so very grateful, and overjoyed to have found the love of my life', or perhaps 'I am delighted and so very thankful that I own a gleaming Mercedes.' Does that make sense?"

"Yes, it does, but why do I have to write those down as if I have them already?"

"Because, my friend, you attract into your life the things you give thought and feeling to on a consistent basis. If you wrote 'I can't wait to have a Mercedes one day', then you begin attracting things into your life that will bring about *waiting* to have a Mercedes. If you wrote 'My soul mate is out there somewhere', you attract situations into your life that will make sure that your perfect soul mate is *out there, somewhere!*"

Pierce smiled and rose to his feet. "The man who wants to be wealthy, should begin at once to act exactly as wealthy people do, to talk as they talk, to work as they do, and more important than anything else, to *think* as they think. Think about your goal as if you had already achieved it and it will surely come to pass. Goodnight. Get some rest. The real trekking begins tomorrow."

PUTTING IT INTO ACTION

On my return to England, I bought a cork noticeboard and began to cut out images from magazines. I bought postcards and searched Google Images for anything relevant I could print out and pin to the board. I added keywords and affirmations, handwritten at first, then typed on my computer and printed out. I later learned how to open the image in Photoshop and place the text on the actual photo (something anyone could do with the free software out there on the web).

The results just blew me away.

The first result was the car I had wanted. It wasn't a Rolls Royce but a car that felt a stretch, yet believable to me. It was a car I'd seen advertised on TV several years before, with full-leather heated electronic memory seats. It also had built-in Sat Nav, folding mirrors, state-of-the-art audio system; it even reported when a tyre had low pressure. Boys and their toys!

Only three months after placing the car on my board, I owned it. Same make, same model, same year, and same colour. Even a few of the registration plate digits were the same.

It came from a friend of mine who used to sell cars on eBay. He'd not been in touch for a long time, and had called out of the blue to catch up. He asked me towards the end of a 30-minute conversation if I still liked this make of car. I told him that I did and asked why he wanted to know. That's when he told me he'd been given one in part exchange. I glanced up from my desk to my vision board, and asked him what colour.

"Gun metal grey," he said.

A chill ran down my spine as I looked at the gun metal grey car on my board.

"Which model? Is it the one with..."

"The top of the range model, Curtis. Sat Nav, electric leather memory seats, on-board computer, the works."

Again, my glance rose to my vision board and those very words that I'd listed on the image.

"Interested?" he asked.

I smiled, with my heart pounding at the possibilities my vision board was presenting. "Interested," I replied.

Shortly after taking ownership of the vehicle, I thought I'd push my luck and add a Rolex watch to the vision board.

Two months later, while driving my beautiful car, and checking the time on my Rolex, I felt giddy with the excitement of it all.

Thoughts really do become things.

I've since built on the whole vision board concept, and now use an electronic version at home.

I still cut out pictures from magazines, print off photos from Google Images, and collect postcards of places I want to experience. The difference now is that I scan them and load them into my vision board software. The keywords ('luxury', 'bliss', 'relaxation', 'success') now get added to a text box on the screen, as are the affirmations ('I am so happy and grateful watching the sun set from my hot tub').

I then select uplifting or inspirational music track from my list, and press the play button. The experience is completely immersive and takes vision boarding to a whole new level. The completed 'movie' is then saved and enjoyed daily.

I recently bought some virtual glasses and watch mine on those before I sleep and first thing in the morning. The goggles create the illusion of watching a 60-inch plasma TV situated ten feet away. Awesome.

My own preference is to use both. Predominantly I use the electronic vision board, but I keep the hard copies in a leather-bound book. Once the dream becomes reality, I transfer the photo to a separate larger book, a 'Book of Achievements', packed with images from the old vision board, with added photos taken when it became real.

You get to the point where you just *know* that the images you're temporarily tacking into the Vision Book will one day be taken out and stuck into the Book of Achievements! It's so exciting. It costs nothing to start the vision board process, and so I recommend you start to do this right away.

Over the next 24 hours, start to think about magazines that might contain suitable images. If you're online, take five minutes to have a quick look at Google Images to see what you can find. The cork board can come later, as can the scrapbooks and ultimately the vision board software. The trick is to make a start.

The Test

I drifted to sleep that night with mixed feelings. My body was being tested—the blisters, breathlessness, aching legs and back—but I was coping.

My mind, however, was split.

On the one hand, it was buzzing with possibility. I'd learned of the ability of my mind to create the future I desired, through relaxation, meditation, visualization, the power of words and pictures.

On the other hand, Pierce's final words still lingered in the room: "Get some rest. The real trekking begins tomorrow."

Real trekking? Was he playing with me? I suspected the ascent of the mountain was about to become even more difficult.

Had I realized how hard it was going to get, I'd have turned around and headed back.

Luckily, I didn't, for what my wise mountain guide revealed to me the next day changed me forever.

CHAPTER FOUR

"I can no other answer make but thanks,
And thanks; and ever thanks."
— **WILLIAM SHAKESPEARE** *(1564–1616),*
TWELFTH NIGHT

Gratitude

I opened my eyes to bright daylight, feeling that I'd overslept. "Good morning," said Pierce softly from across the room. "It is a fine day for it."

I sat bolt upright, startled that he was in my room; I hadn't heard the door open. I scrambled for my watch as Pierce slowly came into focus.

"Have I slept in?" I asked. "What time is it?"

"Worry not," he replied. "You have enjoyed a much needed rest and the day is still young. Over there is your breakfast, if you are hungry."

He gestured to a cloth bundle in the corner.

It turned out that not only had I remained sleeping while Pierce entered my room, I had also slept through the delivery of my breakfast! The temple guy must have knocked on my door and tried not to wake me as I slept.

Pierce opened the door and more light forced my eyes to squint. "I shall hand back your privacy, my friend, let you eat and dress in peace and quiet. Shall we meet by the front gates in, shall we say, half an hour?"

"No problem," I replied. "See you in half an hour. Thanks, Pierce."

As I dressed and ate fruit, I glanced outside to observe the temple for the first time in daylight. Each wall was painted a pale yellow colour, which I hadn't noticed the previous evening by the light of the flaming torch. The builders had used yellow paint, as if the walls had been whitewashed and then a thin yellow wash rubbed over them. The whole place glowed in the morning sun, a clear blue sky adding beauty and serenity to the scene.

By the time I headed to the main gates to meet my guide, I felt fantastic. I still had one or two blisters with fresh plasters and socks over them, and my back and legs were still stiff, but my nose was completely clear and I could breathe through it at last. Life felt good.

As I reached the gate, a small temple worker dressed in yellow robes bowed and began to open the large wooden door.

"'Morning. I was going to wait for my friend here," I said, feeling a little embarrassed that he might have to close the heavy door while I waited.

The man apologized in whispers, explaining that he had not been around when we arrived last night. "I understood we had only one guest last night, sir. My apologies."

"That's OK," I replied. "I arrived with my guide, but he stays with some of you guys. He's not in the same room as me."

Through the gap in the half open door, I was surprised to see Pierce across the way with his map out, making notes and putting an old compass back in his pocket. He saw me and waved.

"Sorry, my mistake, that's him over there. Thank you very much for your hospitality."

"You are very, very welcome, my friend. Take much care on the mountain today. I sense snow in the air."

'Snow'? I thought. The guy was nuts! The sky was blue, the sun shining. What was he talking about?

Off We Go

As Pierce and I ascended through the howling blizzard an hour later, I could feel my nose starting to freeze in spite of the balaclava I wore. Both walking sticks penetrated the deep snow and my legs screamed at me to stop, but it was so, so cold in the icy wind that I just had to keep going.

Pierce kept pushing on like an impervious snow plough. He went over the crest of a hill and down into another snowy valley, his long wooden staff bashing the snow in slick rhythmic motions like the paddle of a canoeist negotiating white water rapids.

The path downhill started to hug a vertical wall of rock and ice to our left, then it arced left and the blizzard intensified. The winds picked up, the snow blew sideways, and visibility dropped to about 30 feet. Suddenly Pierce turned to me and gestured for me to hurry, quickly waving his arm as if there was a problem.

I gritted my teeth and lengthened my stride to catch up. Pierce was pointing at what looked like a cave entrance. The interior of the cave was smaller than the grand entrance, but it was high enough to stand in without stooping and blissfully deep enough to be completely out of the wind and snow.

A few flat rocks at the back of the cave became our armchairs, so we took off our packs, shook off the snow, and sat down with a deep, thankful sigh.

"I can't tell you how happy I am to see this place, Pierce. I tell you, I was so cold, and my legs were killing me."

Pierce nodded and grinned. "It feels wonderful, does it not?"

"Yes, it actually feels warm after being exposed to the elements like that, like we…"

"I meant," Pierce interrupted with a raised eyebrow, "that the gratitude feels good. It is magnificent to look around you, to take in your surroundings, and to be grateful for them, no?"

"Well, yes, I guess so."

"A few days ago, on that rope bridge over the ravine, it looked to me like you were taking a moment to take everything in, to be happy and grateful. Am I correct?"

"Yes, I was very happy and content at the time."

"That feeling of gratitude is one of the most important feelings in the world. It truly is. If you could bottle it and sell it on, you would be a millionaire overnight. Yet, if you harnessed the power of your own personal gratitude and gave it freely, you could be a billionaire in the blink of an eye."

I paused to reflect for a moment as I went into my rucksack for an extra layer of thermal clothing. I didn't fully understand. "I know that it's polite to be grateful and that we shouldn't take things for granted but…"

"Exactly. Most people take the life around them for granted, and focus instead on the things they do not have. A newlywed couple might live in a small apartment dreaming of a house, while taking no time to enjoy their cosy home. Yet they will one day look back on it with the fondness of happier, youthful years.

"When they move into a house, they start dreaming of a larger house for their recent family, taking little time to enjoy the home they sought. They are distracted by bills, appointments, school runs, earning a living, and the hustle and bustle of everyday life.

"If only they had stopped, paused, and enjoyed their children! Enjoyed that home which the children will always look back on with such fondness."

I suddenly felt homesick. He was right.

"You see, at the risk of repeating myself," he continued, "you attract into your fabulous life the things you think about consistently. With enough thought, with enough intent, the feelings push through from your weak conscious mind to your infinitely powerful subconscious mind. Once the seed is planted in the fertile soil of your subconscious mind, you must water the seed, you must take action, but the thought will become reality, as sure as spring follows winter.

"Be grateful then. Feeling happy and grateful puts you into a frequency of appreciation that must, by the laws of this Universe, be reflected back to you. As you are thankful you attract even more things, people, encounters and experiences to make you happy and grateful. Sending out more happy and grateful vibes attracts to you even more happy and grateful events, and on it goes my friend, quickly transforming your life into one fantastic holiday on planet Earth."

What he said made sense.

I pondered a while, while the snow and wind whistled around the cave entrance. It was easy to reflect on my discomfort only minutes earlier, and then be thankful for my present comfort in the shelter of the cave.

I realized that I did, on occasion, take time to appreciate my present circumstances, but not very often—usually when I was in a very comfortable situation following a hard day.

One happy memory that sprang to mind was the time we filmed the Viking movie *Beowulf & Grendel* in Iceland. The set was on a freezing, windswept mountain, so working conditions were often cold and difficult. We used to relax after a hard day's slog, sitting outside in the dark, in a hot tub that was naturally heated by volcanic action below.

Ignoring the slightly 'eggy' sulphurous scent, it was fantastic to lean back with friends as the boiling hot water eased our muscles, while the aurora borealis danced across the star-filled sky. We would look at each other with large smiles, happy and grateful to be unwinding in such indulgent surrounds after being so cold all day at the top of the mountain.

In those situations I did appreciate my life, and admittedly, life was wonderful. However, for the rest of the time, I tended to focus more on where I was going rather than where I was in the moment. It all changed that day in the cave, halfway up the mountain.

"The blizzard seems to be easing," Pierce said, rising to his feet and arching his back where he'd started to stiffen.

"Do you reckon?" I asked, quite comfortable where I was.

"Come," he said, throwing on his backpack and adjusting his hat. "We can set up camp before the afternoon if we keep going."

I rose swiftly and followed him out of the cave, adjusting my rucksack and clipping my chest strap into place. That's when it hit me. Camp?

I wanted to shout out at him, "Camp? In this weather?" Yet, that's what I'd signed up for. I'd fully expected to be camping in tents when I set out. However, after several nights in comfortable temples, I'd grown accustomed to a roof over my head, hot food and a bed!

Here was another example of how I had taken something for granted. Then my positive mind regained control of my thoughts. It could always be worse: imagine being stuck up there *without* a tent. At least we had all the right gear with us, and I had a real mountain expert as a companion.

Beyond the Cave

The wind lessened and the snow ceased as we climbed higher and higher. It became harder to breathe as the oxygen in the air lessened, but the visual rewards spurred me on.

We stopped after a continuous hour of ascent and turned to look back down the mountain. The morning sun lit a carpet of cloud below us as far as the eye could see. Clouds below, and the bluest sky you could ever imagine above.

Complete silence.

"Beautiful, is it not?" smiled Pierce, wiping his nose with his gloved hand.

"It is," I replied, as I regained my breath. "It is."

"Imagine, for a moment, what people back home will be doing today. They reluctantly rise a little late to consume a rushed breakfast, only to rush through traffic to get to the job they only do to pay the bills until the next holiday. Look around you, and see what they are missing. Yet they choose the daily commute. Be thankful that you are here, and not with the masses right now."

I nodded. "I am Pierce, I really am."

Gratitude filled my every cell as we continued to plod higher still through knee-deep snow towards the top of the next ridge.

As the going became tougher, my legs screamed out for me to stop. I battled on, using the breathing techniques taught by Pierce only days previous.

The slow plod up the steep snowy slopes gave plenty of time for me to reflect once more. I began to feel homesick for the simple pleasures, like hugging my daughter and smelling her freshly washed hair out of the shower—a little towel-wrapped bundle of joy. Or the belly laughs as I wrestled with my son, maybe lifting up his little T-shirt and blowing a raspberry on his belly. Or cuddling up with my wife by the roaring fire with a good book, or a tray of nibbles and a classic film.

Simple pleasures.

Heavenly Movies

I'm a fan of movies where people go to heaven or meet angels. I especially like the ones where they are given a glimpse of how life would be without them, or shown how life would have been had they walked a different path.

The Christmas classic *It's a Wonderful Life* is a good example. A desperate George Bailey (played superbly by James Stewart) considers suicide, only to be taken under the wing of trainee angel, Clarence. The angel, played by Henry Travers, gives Bailey a 'glimpse' of what life would have been like for everyone had he not been born. George discovers what a positive impact his life has had on his family, friends, and even the town around him.

In a similar vein, one of my other Christmas favourites is *The Family Man*. Nicolas Cage plays Jack Campbell, a high-flying New York executive who has hit the big time and lives what he perceives to be the perfect life.

In his youth, his fiancée, played by Téa Leoni, asks him not to go to London, where an internship awaits him at Barclays Bank, but to stay with her instead. She feels they would have a magical life together, if only he'd stay. Jack hesitates, but decides to continue his plans, telling her that "Everything will be all right."

Jack Campbell never sees his beautiful fiancée again.

An angel appears whose mission is to show Jack exactly what would have happened, had he chosen to stay with his fiancée all those years ago. Nicolas Cage wakes up in a strange bed, with an older Téa Leoni, kids, a dog and a normal suburban American lifestyle. It's a lovely feel-good film.

You can't help but look around you after watching those movies, and be grateful for your life, and everyone and everything that is part of it.

First Glimpse

"Almost there," Pierce shouted back at me. It had been a gruelling morning of mixed emotions. The steep ascent had taken us through a blizzard, yet we had pressed on to enjoy zero winds and the bluest of skies. Later on, the freezing wind had picked up and chilled my cheek bones, yet we had later enjoyed complete shelter as we ascended a wall of rock and ice.

We'd taken the rough with the smooth, and luckily, my guide's talk of gratitude had kept my mind occupied for most of the climb. As I neared the top of the ridge to join Pierce that day, I was pleased to discover that it was not a 'fool's summit' but the actual top of this lesser mountain.

"And there she is," said Pierce, pointing ahead and up to the heavens. "At least, you would almost see the top if it was not hidden in cloud."

My heart leapt for joy that we'd reached that point in the expedition where we could see our target. Almost.

Then my stomach sank as I realised the kind of distance we still had to cover. It was a considerable descent into the valley below before we could even begin that final climb to our ultimate goal—the lofty summit that had been my dream for over a decade.

The ridge was cold and windy, and so thoughts quickly changed from the summit to the immediate goal – setting up camp. How far, I wondered, before we stopped for the day?

Before I could ask, Pierce spoke out. "Come," he said. "We're closer to our stopping place than you might think."

We almost glided down the steep snowy banks into the valley, slipping and sliding, barely stopping for breath. At one point I lost control, overtaking Pierce and going too fast to stop as a steep drop saw me jumping eight feet from one section to another.

Although I landed in snow, I hit with my legs straight and absorbed the shock in my lower back, which was already aching.

I gritted my teeth and turned to Pierce to complain about the pace. Then I saw him standing, chin and eyebrow raised, like a school teacher waiting for a swear word, yet hoping not to hear one. His expression made me hesitate.

"I am pleased you chose not to curse," he said. "I know you are tired and aching, but you have a lot to be thankful for, my friend. There is a saying in these parts about the man who complained bitterly because he was so poor that he had to walk with no shoes. He complained daily, until he met the man with no feet."

Within the hour, the snow had lessened from knee deep to ankle deep, from powder to ice, and we began to see patches of rock beneath our feet.

By the time we'd turned a rocky corner and descended further still, the ground had become dry under foot and our passage very sheltered from the winds. I began to warm up as the pace lessened. Then a strange sight filled my vision.

Imagine a child's drawing of two mountains side by side. Two triangles of 60 degrees, forming the letter 'M'. Now imagine that a rock the size of a house has fallen from the top of one of these mountains and settled between the two, leaving just enough room for a person to crouch and pass under. As we neared the giant boulder, I realized it was much larger than a house. The rock formed a natural tunnel that went on for several hundred feet.

"Watch your head here," Pierce echoed, as he crouched a little further, bent double at the centre point of this dark passage.

My lower back began to grumble with the continued stooping, as did my tired legs, but my spirits were raised by Pierce's next comment.

"Our home for this evening," he said, a mere silhouette against the circle of light.

Home for the Evening

We were looking down on a small village on the valley floor. A hundred feet above the village, up a rocky slope, lay a wonderful temple, its pale green walls glistening in the north-facing sunshine.

Less than two hours before we had been standing knee deep in snow at the top of a cold windy ridge. Yet here we were, about to enter a village protected from the elements and warmed from the sun in the north—a most unexpected little haven.

As we neared the first buildings, we were greeted with a nod from two local men who had been sitting outside their whitewashed homes. The men got up and stepped inside without a word. The homes here were built very well, with a curious pale green tinge to the whitewash. I noticed the houses were kept very clean and tidy, with pinkish shutters adorning the narrow windows.

Ahead of us, two men were engaged in heated debate. As we neared and they caught sight of us, they lowered their voices and parted company.

"Seems a wonderful little place this, Pierce," I observed. "But are we welcome here? The few people I've seen appear a little uptight."

"One is always welcome at the temple, my friend," he replied. "What you see is simply a place that attracts few visitors, hidden away as it is from the outside world. I see a place forgotten by time, where the inhabitants have grown a little impatient. I witness a lot of anxiety whenever I pass through this village."

"That's a shame," I replied. "I think it's great to be tucked away like this, all self-contained and safe from outside interference."

"Quite," Pierce agreed, waving at a little girl who popped up into view from behind a stack of clay jars. "But it is only when we experience the bustle of life away from this mountain range that we can truly appreciate the serenity of this location. They do indeed have much to be grateful for."

As I walked up the hill to the green temple I felt a little like a spoiled child. Back in the blizzard earlier that day, I had been sure we'd be staying in tents from now on. Yet here we were—Pierce had found us another temple on the mountain. I felt so happy and grateful to be walking and learning with Pierce, and so very thankful for the prospect of a warm meal and a roof over my head.

The temple was built much more substantially than the others I'd seen so far. Its smooth plastered exterior mirrored the colour scheme of the village below, with its pale green wash reminding me of mint ice cream. The four arches that held up the front of the temple were painted pink, and carved with various magical symbols.

"A lot of these symbols relate to matters of the heart," Pierce explained, before I could ask the question.

He then raised his wooden staff and gestured to a copper door knocker. I rattled it on the wooden doors that guarded the entrance. I cringed slightly at how hard I knocked on the door; it was so peaceful here that the sound echoed loudly around the valley.

The doors opened inwardly to reveal a stocky, bald-headed man wearing dark green robes who looked at me intently.

"Hello," I said with a smile. "I'm hoping you might be able to…"

"Enter," said the man, with a large grin. "You are most welcome."

Sanctuary

I lay on the most comfortable bed imaginable. After the morning I'd had, I felt like 'the cat that got the cream'.

Pierce had left me in order to scout the path we'd take the next day. He'd become aware of a rock fall or avalanche that might block our path, and so wanted to take a look. I was fortunate to have such an expert mountain guide.

I was left to relax on my bed, with a stomach full of wonderful food, feeling very happy. I was really enjoying these temple stops. How unusual that the temples were getting ever so subtly grander as we ascended! For some reason, I thought the opposite would be true, and that the higher the temple, the harder it would be to drag materials up the mountain. Clearly this was not the case.

I felt better that day, not only mentally, but also physically. My cold had now completely disappeared—no more runny nose—and the terrible cough and headache from a few days previous were now just a distant memory. I was also pleased with the way my foot care had been going. I'd bought a new kind of blister treatment before the trip, and that seemed to be paying off.

My legs still ached and my back still throbbed, but lying on that bed in blissful silence, it didn't seem to matter. I wasn't even bothered about the slight breathlessness that remained my constant companion. It had been a great few days, and I was now nearer to the top than I was to the bottom.

It felt as though I'd been climbing for much longer than four days. Amazing, I thought, how much life we can cram into a single day when we plan tomorrow in detail, rise early, and make it happen.

I placed my hands behind my head and began to ponder the things that Pierce had mentioned that day. I drifted into a restful afternoon nap, thinking of how gratitude, coupled with visualization, had allowed me to achieve things in life that I'd thought impossible only months before.

| Dragon's Breath |

The medieval banquets got me my initial 'probationary' Equity Card. The *full* Equity Card, which was required by anyone applying to join the Stunt Register, was something quite different.

For this I had to show contracts for approximately 30 weeks of work. Performing a weekend banquet counted as 'half a week', so plodding along as I was, it was going to take me 60 weekends—over a whole year working every single weekend. The snag was that in the summertime, the banquets were much less frequent, certainly not every week. I was going to have to do more than medieval banquets at weekends.

Within a few short months of joining the Pavanne Promotions team to sword fight at medieval banquets, I began to add to my list of skills. To be completely honest, this was driven largely by finances; I noticed the court jesters were paid more than twice what the sword fighters were paid!

They also seemed to have more fun during the banquet: playing the fool, flirting with the girls, making the guests roar with laughter. Then they had their own variety slot towards the end of the evening. It was nearly always the jester who got the greatest applause at the end of each night.

We had one jester at each banquet, and all of them were already established acts booked from outside. That is, they already did that for a living, and our banquet was one of many gigs they played each year. As such, we didn't always have the same jester. One jester would be an expert juggler and unicyclist, another would lie on a bed of nails, while another would be an expert in eating and breathing fire.

I remembered the documentary about Paul Jennings training to become a stuntman and how he learned to breathe fire. At a live summer show one Sunday morning, I asked one of the jesters to teach me.

It would seem very odd to put paraffin into my mouth, and even stranger to then bring a naked flame anywhere near my lips! However,

I'd already seen it performed up close many times, and never seen anyone injured. First, I was told, you must assess the wind direction! A blade of grass is plucked from the ground and tossed in the air, and your back turned so the wind carries the flames away from you.

Next, I was told to practice with water: pursing my lips tight and blowing the liquid through my lips to turn a stream of water into a blast of water vapour. Once the mist created was large enough, fine enough and long enough, I was given a few final tips before reaching for the paraffin and a box of matches.

The tips were mainly about 'breaking away' from the flame as it ignited and came back towards you. Difficult to explain in words, but quite a natural action when a very hot flame is rolling back towards your face! That was that. I lit a fire brand, put blue paraffin in my mouth, and blew out onto the naked flame. A large plume of fire roared from my mouth.

I was amazed.

Within a few short minutes, I was filling my mouth with as much paraffin as possible, after inhaling as deeply as I could, to blow the largest flame I could possibly muster. To my surprise, the flame was as good as any I'd seen in any banquet act, if not larger.

Back home, I continued to practice my fire skills every day in my back garden, much to the amusement of my neighbours. At every banquet, I watched the jesters more closely than ever. I couldn't juggle, and knew the standard of juggling demonstrated by most of them had taken them many years to master, so I had to come up with my own act.

| Nailing It |

Around the time I was perfecting my fire breathing and working on my own 'jester act', I was shown the Bed of Nails.

It was a bright spring Sunday morning in the grounds of an old stately home, and we were there in our medieval outfits to entertain the crowds. Davey walked around playing his lute, his daughter and friend did some Irish dancing, the jester juggled and made people laugh, and the rest of the group and I performed some kind of sword fight in the central arena.

It was during a break that I was invited to try out the bed of nails. Measuring some five feet in length and three feet wide, on its heavy wooden base the bed stood around four feet off the ground. And it was studded with hundreds of six-inch steel nails. These were real nails; if you threw a melon up in the air to land on the bed, the cold metal spikes would easily puncture its flesh.

I had seen other performers lie on the bed of nails, so I decided to give it a try. I removed my blue surcoat and baggy white medieval shirt, and approached the daunting apparatus. The trick of course, if you can call it a trick, is weight distribution.

I pushed away all thoughts of my internal organs being punctured like the melon and gingerly eased my whole back at once onto the nails. It felt *very* uncomfortable, yet I found myself smiling—I was lying on top of hundreds of sharp nails! I was uncomfortable, but not in pain.

Getting up required some assistance, and I found my lower back was a little vulnerable to the nails. I adjusted my leather belt by twisting it around my waist, so that the small loop my sword normally went into now covered my coccyx. I then tried again. The double thickness leather on my tail bone made all the difference.

I found that I was quickly getting used to the sensation, and so the prospect of having someone stand on me in that position began to seem feasible. Yes, you read that correctly! The 'international standard' for a bed of nails act seemed to require the performer to demonstrate three aspects:

First, after some build up, the performer would lie flat on the bed of nails.

Second, after further build up, a member of the audience would be chosen (usually the lightest) to gently stand on the stomach of the performer as they lay on the bed of nails.

Third, as the finale, a paving slab would be placed on the stomach of the performer on the bed of nails, while a sledge hammer was driven down hard enough to smash the concrete.

It was quite exciting. If I could master the bed of nails, I would have my first 'jester's act'. So I tried everything.

I got on and off the nails until I could do so smoothly. I had Kelly, the Irish dancer, step onto my stomach. As her weight began to press down, I naturally pushed up with my heels perched at the foot of the bed and tensed my upper back muscles to ease the pressure in my lower back. It felt fine for the ten seconds she stood there, and looked a lot worse than it felt.

Finally, my fellow performer Ian was brought in to smash the concrete paving slab on me. He had the unenviable task of swinging down a heavy sledge hammer onto the paving slab, with enough force to shatter it, but not too much or I would be driven onto the nails.

I do remember that first test.

I had been fine about easing onto the bed of nails, and relatively OK with the idea of a person standing on me. I thought I was comfortable with the final flourish, until I lay on the six-inch nails, and the cold, rough paving slab was placed on my stomach.

A few of the other performers from the group gathered around, and I suddenly found myself questioning if I was the correct body for this act. Maybe I should try this again when I'd fattened up a little!

Too late. The smiling supporters counted down from five to one as Ian raised the heavy sledge hammer with a serious look in his eyes.

"Five, four, three, two, one..."

Smash!

The impact hurt. The broken pieces of concrete fell from my body, and before I could fully evaluate the exact location of the pain, I was being helped off the bed to the applause of the onlookers.

"Did it hurt?" one asked.

"Are you OK, mate?" said Ian.

"That looked painful! Rather you than me!" said another.

By the time I'd brushed myself down and gathered my thoughts, I wasn't sure if it actually hurt or not.

"Absolutely fine," I said. "No problem at all."

Davey, stepped forward, grinning from ear to ear. "Then I think we have our new bed of nails man."

| Enter the Black Knight |

Within a couple of weeks, I was performing the bed of nails act in front of hundreds of banqueting guests at Eckington Hall near Sheffield.

I'd also learned some basic escapology tricks from jesters I'd met along the way, and began working that into my new act. I was a huge fan of Houdini, and relished the prospect of rediscovering escape methods, from simple body manipulation to lock picking. Over time, I added my own twists to the escapes, introducing extra ropes, a chair, more padlocks, and more hand and ankle cuffs.

So the act became twofold. I would enter as the mysterious Black Knight alongside the hero of the evening, such as Robin Hood, and help defeat the bad guys.

We'd then take over the banqueting hall, and the real partying would begin. After the next course of food, I'd be invited to entertain the crowds with feats of strength and bravery. The bed of nails, covered in a black cloth, would be wheeled on stage, also hiding an array of chains, ropes, padlocks and handcuffs.

I'd choose a couple of strong-looking guys from the crowd, selected earlier that evening as being a little more sensible and less inebriated than the other men in the room, and bring them on stage.

After checking that all of the items were real, they proceeded to tie me tightly to a wooden chair with the ropes, usually double or triple knotting the ropes together around my legs and wrists. A pair of handcuffs was added, then a set of ankle cuffs, followed by a very long steel chain that was wrapped tightly around my body, arms and legs until I couldn't move. Only my head showed. Around me was a large hoop, which acted as a curtain rail for the seven-foot long heavy black material that hung from it. The compère would take over now, encouraging the crowds to slowly count down with him from ten, as the hoop was raised, the dark curtain hiding me from view.

"Ten, nine, eight, seven..."

The first few seconds were frantic as I exhaled and tried to introduce some slack into the ropes and chains, so that I could work on the locks. I was usually out in seven seconds, and then just ruffled the cloth until the dying seconds, to emerge victorious with one second to go.

Occasionally I'd hit a snag, but one of the assistants holding up the curtain would be watching me. If she didn't get the nod from me, she would just smile at the compère, which meant I wasn't free yet and he would change the count: "Three, two and a half, two and a quarter." I would stick my head up above the curtain, look both ways to see what was going on, and then duck down behind the cloth to finish the job. It got a laugh, and there was a lot of humour in the routine anyway, so we got away with it.

Next up was the bed of nails.

I explained what the bed was all about, demonstrated how sharp the nails were, then began to slowly take my clothes off as the drums began to beat and the crowd began to clap and thump tables.

I was usually on around 10 p.m., and they'd been drinking since 6 p.m., so I usually had quite a rowdy audience to entertain.

I wore a pair of very tight, figure hugging black shorts under a pair of medieval boxer shorts, which were under my usual black medieval tights. There was a certain point in the proceedings where I'd removed my surcoat, boots, socks, shirt, and tights, and stood wearing only the medieval boxer shorts.

The drumming would build to a climax as I held the top of my boxer shorts and looked at the crowd to check if they wanted me to take them off.

Every woman was staring at my crotch! "Off! Off! Off! Off!" they chanted. It was very unsettling.

I was no male stripper though; after the big build up, I'd drop my medieval boxer shorts to reveal the second pair of figure-hugging black shorts. I'd skilfully enhanced what nature gave me with a pair of socks and a carefully rolled handkerchief.

Then, it was onto the bed.

I gingerly eased myself onto the six-inch nails, then as the audience applauded I would jump up from the bed and show them the deep imprints on my back. This got a great reaction from the crowd, because although it didn't really hurt, it did leave large impressions in the skin. Suddenly people realized that there was no trick, that I really was lying down on all of those sharp nails.

Then I had a member of the public stand on me. This began with small pretty girls wearing miniskirts, but as my confidence grew, I built up to asking for the heaviest guy in the room. I really did this, there was no trick—just the power of confidence, of self-belief, and the hundreds of performances to perfect the technique.

For the finale, I introduced a nice twist by adding fire.

Having mostly copied the best parts of numerous jesters acts I'd seen, including jokes and heckler put-downs, it was good to put my own stamp on this act—a stamp that many have since copied and perform to this day.

What I did was have a piece of square cotton, the size of a napkin, soaked in paraffin and placed on the top paving slab. The rag would be lit as the audience gasped and cheered. The drums started to roll as the compère asked for complete silence, and reiterated the immense danger of what was about to be attempted. I said nothing this time, and there was a good reason for that—I had a mouthful of paraffin!

An air of seriousness often took over the crowd, the drunken jeers lessened and then died down to a curious murmur as people scrambled onto benches and tables for a better look.

"Five, four, three..."

The sledge hammer was raised above the head of the executioner.

"...two, one!"

As the hammer fell towards the concrete, I put my chin on my chest and spewed fuel from my mouth onto the flaming cloth at my stomach. An immense fireball rolled over my body, through my legs, and dissipated towards the ceiling.

The crashing hammer sent spark-like flecks of burning cloth into the air as the concrete shattered and rolled from my body to the floor.

The crowd were on their feet, clapping, whistling and cheering as I was pulled off the bed to take a bow.

Grateful Reflection

I smiled at the memories that flooded back to me with vivid clarity as I lay on that comfortable bed, halfway up the mountain.

I recalled the feeling of gratitude and contentment that filled my life back then. Pierce was, yet again, correct in his teachings.

I was tremendously grateful for the friendship and hospitality shown to me by Davey and Karon in those early days. I appreciated the almost instant promotion from background guard to one of the three paid sword fighters.

I was indeed grateful to be able to play the Black Knight with his escapology feats and the daring bed of nails demonstration, and for the eventual high point of playing the jester all evening at countless venues.

I had begun that journey with nothing but an image in my mind. An image formed following a TV documentary where an ordinary guy became a medieval banquet performer and was awarded his Equity Card.

The more I was thankful for, the more that seemed to come my way. I hadn't seen it quite that way until that afternoon in the green temple. This Law of Creation was real.

Each sustained thought sprang from a deep rooted passion that triggered a goal. The goal was visualized many times over in my mind, and strengthened by the imagery I surrounded myself with, by the books I read, by the documentaries and movies I watched, and the people I began to mix with. As my life changed I felt a natural gratitude, never realising that the gratitude was playing such an important part in the creation process.

An Early Evening

A knock on the door startled me. I'd nodded off and the room was in near darkness. My door slowly opened to reveal a temple worker with a cloth-covered plate in one hand, a flickering candle in the other, and a broad friendly smile.

"Your supper, sir," said the man, before bowing and backing out of the room.

"Thank you," I replied. "Thank you ever so much."

Pierce lingered in the doorway, a flickering candle illuminating a smile. The sun was very low in the sky and the air much cooler, as Pierce tiptoed into my room and gently closed the door behind him.

I removed the thin cloth from my supper to reveal a bowl of steaming hot vegetable soup, accompanied by two chunks of warm fresh flat bread.

"Go ahead," Pierce insisted. "You will need all the energy you can muster tomorrow."

He didn't have to tell me twice. Pierce sat down beside me on the bed.

Conversation quickly turned to the day's events and I wasted no time in sharing my memories of learning to breathe fire and to lie on the bed of nails. Pierce listened with a smile, enjoying the company.

Then he mentioned the movies I had told him about during the walk that day—*It's a Wonderful Life* and *The Family Man*. "Those stories are perfect examples of how most people live their lives with little gratitude. It is often when we lose something that we realize how precious that thing was. Your life is no exception."

I nodded in agreement. He rose from the bed to walk towards the door, then paused and turned, his candle flickering and casting eerie shadows.

"Tell me," he said, "when you watch these movies, do you wonder what you would miss if you unexpectedly found yourself in the 'next life'? What if you looked the wrong way as you crossed the street and, hit by a truck, found yourself in the 'hereafter'. What would *you* miss?"

Pierce opened the door and turned once more.

"Think about the things you would miss. All of them. If you could never see, feel, touch, smell, hear or sense them again. Then look out for those things every day of your life, and appreciate them, be grateful for them. And you will live a charmed life.

"Sleep well, my friend. I shall see you in the morning."

"Goodnight," I replied as he gently closed the door. The room fell into a peaceful darkness.

IF ONLY I HAD

Let me ask you, as Pierce asked me, what *you* would miss if it were all taken away from you tonight. If you went to sleep in your bed and awoke next morning to find yourself in the next life, what would you miss the most about the life you'd left behind?

I'm sure at the top of your list would be your loved ones: your spouse or partner, children, nieces and nephews, brothers and sisters, parents, friends. Perhaps you'd suddenly wish that you'd sorted that disagreement out, told that person how you really felt, and wished you'd apologized to the other person for that fallout. A flood of emotions would hit you: *"If only I had..."*

You might then reflect on the things you always intended to do, but never quite got around to doing. Perhaps repairing a leaking pipe, or reconciling with a friend. What about that landmark you always thought you'd see? That book you were going to write? That relative you were going to visit?

There was so much to do, but you thought you had all the time in the world. Now that life is over. Imagine.

What food would you miss? What drinks would you wish you could taste? Imagine the sights, sounds, tastes, smells and feelings that you would miss, if you could never experience them again. All those simple pleasures! Strawberries and cream in a summer garden, the warmth of a roaring fire after a winter walk, your favourite meal lovingly prepared.

How much would you miss these things, if you could never, ever experience them again?

Now imagine that a mistake has been made in heaven—it wasn't your time to die. You can return to Earth or you can stay in the hereafter—the choice is yours. *"Go back!"* you yell. *"I want to live!"*

When you wake up back in your home, able to hug all the loved ones you thought you'd never see again, you burst into tears. *Feel* that relief, that love, and feel how much you would cherish the loved ones in your life.

You, dear reader, have the ability to show that love to your loved ones right now. Why not put this book down for a minute and show them how much you love them! Go hug your spouse, or kiss the forehead of your sleeping child. Go ahead and call someone on the phone and tell them you love them. I'll be right here waiting for you when you're done.

As we near the end of this chapter, I'd like to challenge you to do the same as I have done since my return from that magical mountain trip.

Savour life. Enjoy every moment.

At least once a day, just stop and look around you and be in the moment. Feel the sun on your face, the wind in your hair, listen to the chorus of birdsong, notice the beautiful scent of fresh flowers. Be thankful. Literally, close your eyes and say in your mind, *"Thank you!"*

You attract into your life the things you predominantly think about and you attract these things by what you *feel* about them.

A man might think of his large tax bill and feel terrible, unfairly treated and depressed. A woman with an identical large tax bill, with the same income as the man, might feel good, successful and excited.

The man would be thinking from a place of lack and limitation, his greed blinding him to what he actually has. The woman would be thinking from a place of abundance, perhaps realizing that she has a large tax bill because she's earning so much money now, earning more than she ever has, and life is wonderful.

If you really dig deep you *can* find something to be grateful for in any situation.

Even a seemingly awful tax bill usually means you earned more money last year; that's great! Imagine what you could earn *next* year!

Even a testing situation like hitting traffic on your way home can be appreciated. Instead of swearing and looking at your watch, open the window, take a breath, and look around. You'll probably notice things you never knew were there, because you usually fly past them at great speed, on autopilot.

With this outlook, you really can turn your life around.

Imagine a set of scales with negative thoughts and feelings on one side, and positive thoughts and feelings on the other. By living a life of gratitude, we tip the scales in favour of positive thoughts and feelings.

When the majority of our thoughts and feelings are good, positive, happy ones, we start attracting things into our lives that make us feel good, stay positive, and live an exceptionally happy life.

It all starts now. Right now.

Look around you and appreciate the things you have at this very moment. Be grateful for all the good things you have in your life. Forget the things you don't have yet, and just for now, right now, consider the many things you are so privileged to have.

If you begin to consciously appreciate the good things in your life, you will create a new habit of appreciation, and this habit will attract more and more into your life to be thankful for.

Try it. It costs absolutely nothing, makes you feel great inside, and combined with the other knowledge shared in this book, could change your life completely.

When I chatted with Pierce that night in the green temple, about 'heaven movies' and of visiting the afterlife prematurely, I had no idea that I was going to come very close to meeting my maker the very next morning.

CHAPTER FIVE

*"Everything that happens, happens as it should, and if
you observe carefully, you will find this to be so."*
— MARCUS AURELIUS *(AD 121–180)*

Observe

I opened my eyes to complete empty darkness. Was it the cold that woke me? Just then, a light rap on the door caused me to jump upright in the bed.

"Hello?" I whispered.

The door began to creak open, and I was pleased to behold a temple worker carrying a steaming bowl.

The hot, slightly savoury porridge tasted good, and by the time I'd washed it down with the spicy tea, I was wide awake and ready to make an early start on the mountain.

Venturing out from my temple room, I paused for a moment and looked up to the dark sky above. I'd gone to sleep with thoughts of living a life of gratitude. I smiled as I wiggled my toes to finally find them 'blister free'—facing a trek to the top of a steep mountain after several days of walking it was a blessed relief. My smile broadened to a grin as I surveyed the navy blue sky, the sun just starting to break over the horizon and hidden from view by the mountain silhouette. Above and behind me, the ancient stars twinkled and blinked—so much mystery and wonder.

I breathed in the frosty air through my nose, paused, and slowly exhaled through my mouth. Silently I said *"Thank you."* It was great to be alive.

"Ah," whispered a gentle voice from behind. "The student arrives at class before the teacher!"

"'Morning," I said to Pierce warmly. "I was just taking it all in."

"Indeed, the world is a wondrous place, is it not?"

He stood beside me and inhaled, his eyes closed. He breathed out a long, long breath, opened his eyes, and turned to me. "Come. Let us make a start. If we leave now and climb steadily, we can reach our highest point by midday."

Climbing High, Sleeping Low

We left the silent green temple behind us, slowly ascending the rocky path out of the valley. Pierce shared his plan for the trek ahead.

In whispers, he explained that the morning would be spent ascending the mountain, crossing the snow line once more to an altitude quite close to the height of the summit. The climb would be slow and regular, as the air would be much thinner than it had been so far. After a short time at this altitude, we would then descend, and spend the night slightly lower down the mountain, where the air was richer and aided restful sleep.

In a way, Pierce had been doing this all along, ascending slightly higher and then descending into camp. This is all part of an experienced guide's 'acclimatization' to the altitude. If you were to walk straight up the mountain, you would be more likely to suffer altitude sickness. By climbing high and sleeping lower, your body gets used to the lack of oxygen in the air as you reach for the summit.

Pierce checked his compass, looked pensively at the slope ahead, and then checked it again.

"Fresh snow on ice," he said. "Up ahead. I'm wondering if we can skirt around it."

He pointed out a path along the ridge that led to a steep bank and a snowy rock face that seemed to stretch right up to the wispy clouds near the summit.

His concern seemed to be more about the fresh snow high above us than the route we'd be climbing that morning. With no realistic alternative, he put away his compass and plodded on.

"What's next then?" I asked with a smile.

"Well, we walk along the top of this ridge until we hit the bottom of that peak, then we twist left towards…"

"No, I mean, what's next in your arsenal of wisdom!"

"Oh, I see," Pierce replied with a smile. He stopped and placed his hands on his hips. "Let me see. You are open now to the notion of your thoughts creating your reality. You understand the importance of your thoughts, of thinking in a certain way?"

"I do," I replied, as we slowly began to walk again.

"You understand the importance of visualization, of imagining your goals and desires in absolute clarity? I hope I have stressed the need to visualize these things daily, in relaxed contemplation or meditation."

"Yes, I understand what you have told me, Pierce. It's really made me think differently already, and I'm excited by the implications for when I get home."

"Your gratitude pleases me much. And we discussed appreciation yesterday, did we not?"

"We did indeed."

"When you have truly found your passion, your purpose, and made a note of exactly what you want your future to be, you are ready to begin. When you have formed a clear mental picture, with the help perhaps of a vision board, and written affirmations, you are ready to meditate. When meditating daily, even for just ten minutes to begin with, you can bring about the things you want to have, be or do, directly on the screen of your mind. You can feel the emotion of contentment or happiness, of gratitude for the things you see in your mind.

"When you repeat this process daily, amazing things will begin to happen to you in your life. Amazing things!"

Pierce stopped dead in his tracks, and held his walking stick out to my chest, as if to prod it. "If you did not know better, you might put these things down to 'coincidence' but there are no such things as coincidences. Everything happens for a reason, and the world you witness around you is the result of your thoughts.

"If you amble along in this life," Pierce said as he started walking again, "without consciously creating your own brilliant existence, then you fall into the default creations of the masses. Believe me, those who do not consciously create, need only look about them to understand the mind set of the modern world."

He then went on to describe a world of greed and selfishness, where one country throws away thousands of tons of food while elsewhere tens of thousands starve. A world where the soil is killed by chemicals to cope with consumer demand and animals are force-fed and pumped with poisons. If people are not killing each other in the name of religion, they are chopping up rainforests that are the lungs of this planet or killing whales. If they're not overfishing the ocean, they are dumping chemicals and nuclear waste into it, or spilling oil.

"Do you choose to drift with the masses," said Pierce, "and live in their world of selfish, destructive thoughts and uncharitable desires? Or do you, as I suspect you do, choose to carve out your own world, by altering your perception of it, realizing that you can dramatically change it for the better, and consciously creating a life that until now you could barely dream of?"

The crunch of snow seemed amplified while Pierce awaited my reply. He'd come out with some heavy topics, quite unexpectedly. Until now Pierce had seemed 'out of time', as if he'd been shut away on the mountain for years and not read a newspaper for decades. Yet there he was, fully aware of our predicament all along.

Somehow I wanted to defend myself against his remarks, as if Pierce were an alien visiting our planet, and I the person chosen to represent mankind. Everything he said, though, smacked of truth, and I knew it.

Yet there on the mountain, I was being given an option to make a difference, a chance to take my life in the exact direction I wanted it to go—the option to reject all of the negativity, greed, ego, and replace them instead with kindness, sharing and charity, as I went about creating my perfect life.

"You're right," I eventually spoke out. "I'd choose to create my own life, and a good one at that."

"Then so you shall," he replied. "So you shall."

As I listened intently to my guide on our steep ascent of the creaking ice and snow that day, I couldn't wait to put all of his advice into action. For some reason I didn't doubt anything that Pierce was telling me. It felt like an ancient wisdom was being passed on to me that I knew, deep down in my heart, to be true.

The White Death

"So how do I...?"

"*Shhhh...*" Pierce interrupted. He paused, breathed in, and closed his eyes. *"Something is wrong."*

"How do you mean? What?"

"I'm not certain, and yet... that still, small voice, that gut instinct is telling me to proceed at my own risk, indeed, making me question if we should proceed at all."

A loud crack caused us both to turn and look above us, but there was nothing to see, just a little ice dust bouncing down the ice wall to our left.

"Follow me, quickly!" said Pierce. "This way."

He ventured left from our path towards the rock face, and started to jog along with his left shoulder rubbing the ice.

"Come!" he whispered.

Another loud crack above, and a bang, like a firework or gunshot.

Pierce pulled me towards the mouth of a small cave, barely large enough for four adults to stand in side by side.

"Can you explain to me why we're…"

A rumble of thunder shook the ground we stood on and took the words from my mouth, along with my very breath. The trembling ground became an earthquake, followed by a flash of white, and then nothing.

Silence.

I opened my eyes, confused. Where was I? Had I woken in an igloo or an ice cave? Was I dreaming?

As my aching brain caught up with my senses, I realized that I was buried in snow, with only enough room to rotate my body and move my head back and forth enough to see the ray of light shining in from a small hole above. I instinctively clawed at the frozen snow, and realized that my body was numb. I had lost consciousness, and heaven only knows how long I had lain in my frozen tomb.

I scrambled for the hole of light, no bigger than a football, and punched away at it with my numb fists, until it fell apart and grew large enough for me to climb through. I emerged into a silent, alien landscape of pure white. The path we'd been walking on lay buried in over six feet of heavy snow.

Where was Pierce?

With intense trepidation, I rushed back, head first into the hole. *"Pierce! Pierce!"* I yelled, trying to block any thoughts of having lost him.

I returned to the bottom of the hole, which was mainly the cave we'd stood in, but stuffed with compressed snow. Scratching and kicking, I quickly had to face up to the fact that Pierce was gone. My heart raced and I began to feel sick with fear.

Scrambling back to the surface, I again yelled out at the top of my voice. *"Pierce! Pierrrrrrce!"*

"Hellooooo?" came a faint echo from down below.

I ran towards the sound and squinted to make out a dark shape, moving towards me some fifty feet distant. The unmistakable figure of Pierce emerged, still clutching his staff, and still grinning from ear to ear. "That was a close one, old boy!"

An immense emotion hit me with as much surprise and intensity as the avalanche just minutes earlier. *"You're alive!"* I said, tears welling in my eyes, and a lump the size of an apple forming in my throat. *"I thought you were done for!"*

"I am fine," he said, catching me up, "Fine. And overjoyed to see that you made it out too. I knew something was wrong. You see, had I not followed my instincts, we would be broken bodies many miles from here."

"Yes, I suppose we would be."

Pierce looked up, nodded and began to walk on. "Are you fit enough to pick up the pace a little? We have lost time, and our path will be more hazardous following the avalanche."

With that, he continued to walk and clamber up ever steeper inclines, over narrow ledges, and around giant boulders of ice, as if avalanches were everyday occurrences.

I joined him and just pressed on. I was cold, and I guess I was in shock. The enormity of my close shave with death hit me a little later, as is usually the case. I've had a few 'close shaves' in my life, and it's usually some time before the gravity of the situation sinks in.

Take the last time I went to Africa, for example.

| Snake! |

I'd climbed Mount Kilimanjaro in Tanzania with a friend of mine, and decided to go on safari in Tarangire National Park the following day. The drive to the park by Jeep was interesting and the afternoon filled with some amazing sights, a high point being the discovery of a herd of wild elephants. By the time we arrived at our safari lodge later that afternoon, we were tired and hungry. My friend Tony and I wasted little time in throwing our rucksacks into our bungalows and heading to the posh bar and restaurant.

The food was terrific after ten days on the mountain, and the wine flowed like water, as we celebrated our successful adventure in Africa. After the meal we drank more wine, this time by the bonfire that roared on the terrace overlooking the watering hole down below. As dusk turned to darkness, the African plains burst into life with a chorus of birds, insects, mammals, and things that go bump in the night!

When the wine was gone and the fire burned down, it was time for bed. On the path to our separate bungalows we were joined by a hotel porter, who followed us with a torch.

He saw us to our rooms, we thanked him, tipped him, and bid him "Goodnight."

Tony and I were laughing and chatting as we unlocked our doors, and I'd clearly drunk more than him because he was into his place before I had the key in my lock, and had already shut the door when I stood on the draught excluder.

At least, it felt like a draught excluder. Something sausage-shaped, made of rubber and filled with air.

I knew it was filled with air, because as I stood on it, it hissed loudly, as if I were letting the air out of it.

"What the..."

I opened the door and looked down through blurry eyes to see what I'd stood on—a huge snake, that zigzagged from my door into my bungalow and under my bed!

I'd love to say that 'being a macho stuntman, I dealt with the situation expertly'. But I can't.

In truth, I slammed the door and ran screaming like a small girl to Tony next door. *"Snake! Snake! Tony, there's a snake in my room!"*

Tony came out with a smile on his face. "Yeah, yeah..." just in time to see me go running past his door.

"I'm off to get help," I shouted and jogged to reception.

I explained the situation to the receptionist, but her reaction made me doubt myself. I was describing a snake as thick as my forearm and around five feet long, but she made gestures about a grass snake, and laughed.

"No, seriously," I said, "I need someone to come take a look."

The receptionist beckoned to a night porter, had a quick conversation in whispers, and he began to laugh too, making the shape of a cobra with his hand and asking in broken English if it were a small cobra.

Although quite intoxicated at the time, I sobered up for a moment at the thought that cobras were an accepted accompaniment to the guests' rooms.

Eventually, and with reluctance, the porter picked up a small stick and a can of spray, and asked me to show him the snake. When I got back to the bungalows, Tony was waiting, flinching at every sound he heard and throwing light on anything that seemed to move.

"Are you serious?" he said to me. "A snake in your room?"

"Yes, I stood on the bloody thing!"

The porter tiptoed into my room, yelled, jumped on a table, and then slammed the door.

From our vantage point outside the bungalow, we watched the silhouette of a frightened man, prodding, spraying, knocking bedside lamps over, and slipping on furniture.

"Do you need help?" I asked from behind the window, expecting him to tell me he was fine and that he'd got the snake.

Instead he replied, "Yes, bring more help. Tell them it is puff adder."

I ran back for more help, and it took three of them in the end to catch and kill the snake. A part of me felt bad to see it held by its head, dead, its body dragging along the floor from the man's shoulder height. Another part of me was relieved it was all over.

By the time I fell into bed, I was shattered. I was asleep before my head hit the pillow. I didn't hear Tony next door, nervously checking every cupboard, drawer, and under his bed for spiders and snakes!

When I awoke the next morning, with the mother of all hangovers, I decided to opt out of the early morning safari we'd booked, and instead let Tony go off by himself. I drank water and waited to feel human again in the foyer of the hotel. There I read for the first time the large notices that we had failed to spot the afternoon we arrived: "This park is frequented by dangerous wild animals. Never stray from the paths, never head to your room without an armed guard, and *never* go out after dark or head to your room in the dark."

Oh dear.

I learned in a conversation with our safari driver later that day that the puff adder I had trodden on was deadly. The cause of many deaths, the snake is responsible for more fatalities than any other snake in Africa! Its bite is so strong that its fangs can pierce leather boots—I'd stood on it with walking boots and wearing a pair of shorts!

I later read that the venom happens to be the most toxic of any viper. A typical venom yield for this snake is between 100mg and 350mg. The consensus is that 100mg is enough to kill an average adult man. The average puff adder has enough venom to kill four men.

I actually stood on it, and it hissed very loudly, usually a sign that it was about to strike.

For once, the drunken stupor had been useful—it had saved my life. Had I been sober, I'd have jumped back and screamed, and the thing would have bitten me. Instead of recoiling, I'd mistaken the hiss for the expressing of air from a rubber draught excluder and then casually opened the door.

I can only guess that my gargantuan size 11 boots had hurt the poor creature as it slept, and when I opened the door it opted for the dark beneath the bed as a safe haven.

Hindsight

Sometimes you have a close brush with death, but don't see it that way until you look back in hindsight. So it was with the snake, and likewise, that's how it was with the avalanche that day on the mountain.

Pierce had heard a small voice in his head that told him to stop, to pause for a moment. He recognized the crack above as ice shifting, and sensed the danger, running to the rock face for cover, and beckoning to me as he spotted a slight cave in the rock face. Had he not listened to his intuition, the full weight of that snow and ice fall would have flattened us into the ground.

And so it was that we carried on, Pierce striding boldly as if nothing had happened, and me following along, forever looking up at any snow on the slopes above, wincing at the slightest crack or pop of ice above us.

It was with great relief that I eventually reached the ridge that would be our highest point above sea level that day. With the nearest peak some miles distant, there was also no risk of avalanche from above. The snow beneath our tired feet was firm; we could be sure it would not slide out from under us.

The air was thin, and I felt slightly light-headed. It was also very still, and so we were warm and happy to eat some bread and fruit, looking out over the sea of cloud that stretched out as far as the eye could see.

The occasional summits of lower mountains poked through the carpet of cloud, dark skeletal fingers pointing upwards to the silent frozen heaven.

"We were lucky back there," I said to Pierce.

"Lucky?" he replied, lifting his woolly hat to scratch his head.

"I mean, the chances of being near that cave when the snow came down—a million to one."

Pierce looked confused. He looked at his boots for a moment, then looked up at me and stared deep into my soul.

"That was not luck, my friend. We create our own luck, our own opportunities. Have I not told you so already? Nor are there 'coincidences'. I stopped believing in those many, many years ago. We create our world with our thoughts and actions. Everything in your life began with a thought. You would not be here now had you not thought of this mountain in the first place."

I frowned.

"Did you not think of this mountain before coming here?"

"Kind of."

"Go ahead," Pierce smiled. "I am all ears."

The Dusty Bookshop

I swallowed a piece of mango. "Well, this mountain isn't in any guide books. So I did imagine this *kind* of mountain, yes, and I did know which part of the world I'd find it, but I didn't know about this exact mountain from the start.

"I thought about the kind of mountain I wanted to climb, off the tourist track, in a spiritual, tranquil part of this continent. Then I was in a second-hand bookshop in York just a week or so later, when I literally kicked over a stack of books on the floor upstairs.

"One book caught my eye. It was an old book written in the days of the British Empire, an explorers' book, and when I opened it I saw a sepia photo of the mountain range we're on now. I knew right away that this was the place I was going to visit, and had found my mountain."

"Interesting," Pierce replied, standing more upright with both hands perched on his staff. "You visualized a mountain, but *felt* it had to be in this part of the world, tranquil, spiritual, and off the usual tourist trail?"

"Yes."

"And then, quite by chance, you discovered exactly what you were looking for in an old bookshop, in the pages of a book written some 150 years before?"

"Well, yes, that's right. Things like that happen to me all of the time."

"And they happen to me too. And to everyone else. Everyone that is open to seeing them."

"How do you mean?"

"Do you really believe the book that landed at your feet did so by pure chance? Do you really believe that it had nothing at all to do with your thoughts the previous week?"

"Well, I'd like to think that…"

"Believe it, my friend, for it is true. I tell you, there are no such things as coincidences. It is the Universe at play, bringing to you by default the very things that you hold in your mind repeatedly.

"You sent out the vibration of this spiritual, peaceful mountain in this part of the world, and your vibration was matched, returning to you people, places and events to draw you to this place.

"What drew you to York that day?"

"I don't remember. I like it there, I've been going there for years and…"

"What drew you to the old bookshop?"

I paused to think, but couldn't answer.

"What caused you to be distracted enough to knock over the books? What caused the bookstore owner to put *that* book on *that* pile in *that* place? Indeed, how did the book even end up at that bookstore after travelling from bookshelf to bookshelf for 150 years?

"There are no coincidences, and the moment you accept this you notice a magic to life that is as real as anything you can see, hear or touch. You begin to live a powerful, magical life where you see, more and more, the connection between your desires, your thoughts and these opportunities that land at your door.

"We arrived at that cave because my intuition told me to proceed with caution. My ears became supersensitive to the sound of cracking ice, and as I have finely tuned my senses over the years, I knew I had to go to the wall of ice and head along it quickly.

"It therefore came as no surprise to find the little cave there, and as I dragged you in when the snow hit, I was giving out untold gratitude to the Universe for leading us to protection.

"Instinct. Inspiration. That 'still, small voice' is real inside every human being on planet Earth, regardless of age, gender, skin colour, religion. We all have it. Only few choose to use it.

"Coincidences, they do not exist. Think of them instead as 'signs' that your creative powers are working, and indicators of the path to follow."

"Yes! I entered the bookshop, found the book and bought it. Then I scanned the sepia photo and stuck it above my desk so I could look at it daily and get excited about going some day."

"Which is precisely how you managed to finance the trip, to find the tour operator and work everything out."

"Yes, everything just fell into place!"

"It would! Because you were training your mind every time you looked at that photo, and acting on 'coincidences' that came your way. I bet if you really thought hard about it, you would recall lots of supposed coincidences leading up to the trip?"

"Yes, there were a few. The cost of the trip was way more expensive than an expedition I'd usually attend alone, and yet a stunt job came in that, although it initially seemed too small to cover any costs, ended up paying ten times my usual daily fee!

"When the cheque arrived, it was for the exact amount needed to pay for this trip. So yes, now that you mention it, a day's work never paid for a holiday like this before, and because it was just a day's wage, I could justify the outlay to my wife!"

Pierce smiled and nodded. "Everything happens for a reason. I hope now that you will see these 'coincidences' for what they really are. Come, let us head down from this ridge. The sun is already getting low in the sky."

Pierce paused to point something out with his stick—a distant peak, its crown hidden in mist.

"We are almost there, you know. The summit beckons," he said. "Tomorrow will be the last time that we climb high and rest low, for the following day we shall reach the summit of this beautiful mountain."

I was so close, yet it seemed so far away above me. My blisters were gone, but I still had a slightly aching back, although I had to admit that it was more my legs now that felt the punishment I had put them through these past few days.

With each downward plod, I imagined what the summit might look like, and felt a huge sense of gratitude for reaching the top. I imagined hugging Pierce, patting him on the back, and raising my arms in the air. It was close now, and I couldn't wait.

Rooftops Below

After the descent through deep snow, we traversed sheets of ice that shone like great skating rinks in the glaring sunshine.

The ice eventually gave way to frozen rock, as we reached a make-shift path that began to spiral up once more, turning clockwise up a natural cone of rock that stood hundreds of feet high.

At the top of the spiral, I was surprised to see a trickle of water running from a frozen icicle. The water fell a few feet to a thin icy stream, which quickly disappeared into a rock on its way downhill. Bits of old rope and frozen cloth were scattered around.

"This is the spring that serves our hosts for tonight," said Pierce. "We are very near."

As the path spiralled down to the left, I caught sight of pale blue rooftops below us. They were very pointed and ornate, and it felt strange approaching from above, looking down over the top of the small village.

"I still find it odd that a village could be so self-contained at such altitude, cut off from everyone else."

"Perhaps it exists here for the very reasons you mention: to be away from the masses, in a place of peace and contemplation. I am sure that is why they built their beautiful temple here. Perhaps the others built up their village around the temple over the years."

It was the smallest village I'd seen so far, but the buildings were smarter, and cleaner, perhaps a little larger than the ones in the last village. The slight scent of incense drifted on the breeze to greet me. A woman was sitting outside her home, her blue door ajar, nursing her small child, and wearing a thick woollen cloak and brilliant smile. I nodded as I passed, and she returned the gesture in a friendly manner. Other people emerged, some coming out from their houses, others leaning through shuttered windows as the murmuring began. Some of the locals seemed more content here than I'd seen in the other villages, while others seemed a little fed up.

"The mood seems OK here, Pierce. How do you find these people?"

"Oh, they are good people on the whole. For some reason though, a lot of the people in the village are pessimistic. They will assume, for example, that this bright sunny weather will be over very soon. Perhaps others will assume the sun will stay too long, drying out the crops lower down the mountain. The truth is, of course, that the sunny weather today just 'is'—it is neither a break from the rain, nor the start of a drought—it just 'is'. Not many people here would understand that. In the temple, yes, but here in the village, no.

"They could live for the moment, and enjoy the sunshine, feel the warmth of the sun on their face, hear the sound of that babbling brook, and breathe in the cool fresh air through their nostrils. Breathe it in and enjoy it.

"If only the people in this village could do that, they would realize that they already had everything they could ever want, and more, and are the creators of their own destiny."

We turned from the main row of buildings and there before us stood a sight to behold.

A Host With the Blues

The temple was surprisingly grand. Larger than the one we'd left that morning, its rugged exterior was made from great stones that had been fitted together with skill and ingenuity.

The walls had been whitewashed, and then painted over in a pretty sky blue colour, which looked stunning in the late afternoon sun.

We stood between two imposing columns that held up the triangular roof of the entrance, forming an arch and carved from a light wood that seemed to have been there for centuries. Walking forward through the archway, we approached two large wooden doors adorned with magical symbols.

Pierce gestured towards a thick, blackened rope that hung to the left of the doors. When I tugged at the rough rope, there was no audible sound, and yet moments later, the doors slowly and silently began to swing inwards, to reveal a cobbled courtyard with lots of doors leading off into various chambers.

We walked through the large entrance, and it was only as the doors slowly closed behind us and clunked to a halt that a temple worker appeared.

Small in stature, very thin, his blue garments hung from his delicate frame like the clothes of an adult being worn by a child playing 'Mums and Dads'.

"Welcome," he said in a whisper. "Will you be joining us for the evening?" His accent was heavy, but his English excellent.

"If that's OK, thank you."

Pierce hung back as the worker started to lead me across the courtyard, and we passed through a room full of candles and burning incense. There I saw people sitting quietly, some cross-legged, some kneeling, all with their eyes closed, and all looking totally serene. We passed through some heavy rugs that covered a door frame, and came to a small hut. The spindly man bowed to me with his hands clasped in front of him, as if praying, and I returned the gesture.

"Will you take supper with us?" he asked, stepping back from the door.

"Yes, please. Can I eat here, or do I have to come and eat with you and your friends in a different building?"

"As you wish," he replied, looking slightly disappointed. "I will bring food to you later."

I felt bad because he had misunderstood me. All I meant to ask was if he was happy for me to eat with the others, or if he preferred for me to eat in my room. From his facial expression, I realized right away that he had invited me to join him and the temple workers, a real honour, and I had asked instead to eat alone. Oops! Before I could correct the mistake, he had bowed once more and left the area, allowing me to step into my room for the night.

Shutting the door behind me, I glanced around the room with a smile. The interior was adorned with smooth plaster, painted a similar sky blue colour to the outside walls, perhaps a little lighter.

It had more wooden furniture than the place I'd stayed the night before, and the bed looked slightly longer—long enough to fit into without my feet sticking out of the end! Until that night, I'd had to sleep in a foetal position, because had I straightened my long legs, they'd have poked out over the end of the bed. I'm six feet two inches tall, and the people in this part of the world are, for the most part, quite small.

So it was with great joy that I slipped off my boots and jacket, and crept under the covers to stretch my legs. As soon as my head hit the tube-shaped cushion that was my pillow for the night, I realized how very tired I was. I also realized that my backache had finally gone and, because I'd just descended from the higher ridge, I could inhale much more deeply. Wonderful!

I wiggled my tired toes beneath the blankets as my eyes rolled backwards in my head. My warm calf muscles and thighs tingled with delight. I melted back into the comfy bed, my whole body buzzing in beautiful bliss.

| Coincidence in Action |

As I relaxed and allowed my mind to wander, I thought back to the day's events. Surviving the small avalanche was the first thought that came to mind, and how fortunate we had been to get away so lightly.

I got to thinking about 'coincidences', and how they might have played a more significant part in my life than I'd have thought at the time.

I mentioned to you already that my first bid to gain the elusive Equity Card was via the medieval banqueting route. I grew up in the northeast, in a place called Ormesby, which is five miles or so from the industrial town of Middlesbrough. While Ormesby had a lot going for it—a few minutes' walk onto the rolling hills and a short drive to the coast—it lacked the opportunity to perform to the public, and get paid for it.

So I looked at a map on my bedroom wall, and measured halfway between Ormesby and London (where I correctly assumed most of the work in TV & film would be). The map pin pressed into Nottingham, some 125 miles away, and within a week I was in the city centre, with a local newspaper in my hand, circling 'Flats To Let'.

At this time in my life, I was going to church every Sunday. It was a 'minority' church with a small congregation; it certainly wasn't the Church of England. I only regularly went to church for a couple of years, but I'm glad I did because it switched back on a spiritual light bulb that had been switched off in my childhood, a bulb that has remained lit ever since, shining brighter and brighter with each passing year.

I'm not religious now. I'm very spiritual, but at that time of my life, from being 21 years of age, it did me the world of good. I prayed I would be able to find a branch of the church in Nottingham, and 'fit in' as I had in Middlesbrough. I imagined what the church might look like, and how I might socialize with my new Nottingham church-going friends.

I finally filled my car with all of my worldly goods and arrived at my new home in a part of Nottingham called Radford. Minutes after unpacking, I decided to go for a walk to get my bearings and found myself in the sports centre, where I saw a poster for a trampolining club operating that evening.

"Perfect!" I thought. "I can carry straight on with my trampolining training, and it's walking distance from my flat!"

That evening I went along to the club, where a man was setting up the trampoline. He introduced himself as Paul, and was the first person I'd actually spoken to in Nottingham.

When Sunday arrived, I drove to a place in Nottingham called Bulwell, where the Nottingham branch of my church was. On the way there, nervous at the prospect of walking into a church full of strangers, I spotted a familiar face in a car that pulled up alongside me. It was Paul, the trampolining instructor! Not only that, but for 15 minutes I followed him until he turned into the church car park!

He invited me to sit with him, introduced me to his friends, and the cogs of the Great Machine continued to turn. Within three months, Paul ended up being my landlord in a lovely part of Nottingham called Sherwood. It was thanks to him that I met Riky Ash, another trainee stuntman who was to become a close friend over the years.

Lying in my cosy bed in the temple, I gave the memories some real serious thought. 'Something' had prompted me to go for a walk when I first arrived in Nottingham. This then, was an example of what Pierce meant by 'listening to that still, small voice'. I did it intuitively at the time; I 'felt' the need to go for a walk and get my bearings, and resisted the opportunity to be lazy and stay in the flat.

I 'felt' the need to check out the trampolining club for myself, that very night. I 'felt' like going to church, even though I was shy and worried I might not fit in. By following the sequence of events my heart was leading me to, I made lots of friends, attended church, and became a skilled trampolinist.

In the temple bed, I fluffed up my pillow and got comfy once more, while another string of coincidences came to mind, those that led me to playing Robin Hood at *The Tales of Robin Hood* in Nottingham.

A few months before leaving Ormesby for Nottingham, I'd actually got a job (or so I'd been told) at a nearby Wild West theme park called The American Adventure—Western riding, gunfights, falling from rooftops, fist fighting in the saloon. I couldn't wait! The theme park didn't open until Easter and the rough plan was to get a job nearby to keep me going until then.

I'd seen a job going at a swimming pool in a town called Loughborough. The leisure centre was advertising for lifeguards, and I happened to be a qualified lifeguard as part of my water-based stunt training. As it happened, a new teacher to the school I was working in was from Loughborough, so he was able to explain how well situated the town was for my needs. Then I mentioned the Loughborough pool to a close friend of mine one random Saturday.

"That's weird," he said. "My sister lives in Loughborough, and I'm going to see her tomorrow. Do you want to come with me, maybe check out the pool?"

It seemed a long way, so I hesitated before answering, "Yes, why not? I'll come with you."

That one decision forever shaped the course of my life.

I'd found a job I was qualified for, in a town that I'd never heard of a few months before, and a teacher had just moved 140 miles north to Middlesbrough from that same town, to work in the same department as I worked.

Coincidence? Maybe.

Furthermore, a good friend of mine just 'happened' to have a sister in the same town.

The next 'coincidence' occurred the following day, during the visit to Loughborough. My friend's sister had just been to a medieval banquet in Nottingham. Not only that but her best friend was the wardrobe mistress, and her sister was married to the director Davey, who lived in the next village, Barrow upon Soar.

A nervous chat on the phone, a mention of my being a sword fencing instructor, and before I knew it, I had an audition arranged for the following Saturday! I laughed aloud at the memory, and at my stupidity for not thinking more of the coincidences at the time.

I thought long and hard from my temple bed. What were the chances of my friend visiting his sister for the first time in years, the day after she'd been to her first medieval banquet, where her friend from the next village made the costumes, who was the sister of the director's wife, who was looking for actors, who signed me up, and whose show got me my Equity Card which opened the door for me to do TV work?!

Billion to one? Pierce was right, of course. There are no coincidences.

The job at the Wild West theme park, The American Adventure, didn't happen that year. Had I decided 'not' to go to Loughborough that day, I'd have been well and truly stuffed!

I did eventually get the chance to work at the theme park the following year—as the Sheriff of Silver City. I protected the town from bad guys, who'd ride in to rob the bank. I had a lot of dialogue, which was good experience, got dragged down the street behind a horse, had a fistfight and shot a baddie down from the roof with a shotgun. Great fun!

Misunderstanding

"Food!" shouted a man outside the door of my room, followed by a loud knock. *"Food!"*

I jumped up from the bed, bleary-eyed, and opened the door. It was the same thin man I'd met earlier. He still seemed upset that I wanted to eat alone.

I considered explaining myself more clearly as I took the tray from him, but he bowed and quickly walked away, barging past Pierce on the way.

"Are you rested?" Pierce asked, turning in amazement to watch the man who had just pushed past him.

"A little. I haven't slept, just been thinking while I relaxed. What about you?"

"Oh, I have been with friends, eavesdropping on conversations and the like," he said with a grin, entering my room and closing the door behind him as I sat on the bed and removed the cloth from my tray.

The wonderful aroma of spicy spinach and potato filled my nostrils, causing my mouth to water in anticipation. The food was excellent.

I explained to Pierce the misunderstanding between the skinny man and myself, and he just laughed, explaining that I shouldn't worry, and that they made allowances for 'Western ways'.

We chatted some more that evening, about intuition and inspiration, until the sun had drifted down over the western ridge that overshadowed the blue temple.

We didn't speak about the next day, for we each knew that a difficult day's trekking lay ahead, and also that the end was finally within our grasp.

ANOTHER LITTLE CHALLENGE

Identify your dreams, surround yourself with images and affirmations, daily meditations, and then...observe.

Watch. Wait. Notice.

You are going to be surprised at just how many apparent coincidences drop right into your lap. This is about looking out for the little signs that point you in the right direction, and acknowledging them.

With practice, you learn to smile at these synchronicities that begin to rise to the surface, like bubbles released on the seabed, and get excited by the number of 'coincidences' that leap out at you and beg for your attention.

Notice these coincidences. Notice noticing these coincidences. You'll need to act on them.

Another thing to look out for is 'inspiration'. As you put into practice what I have been sharing with you these past few days, you will begin to hear that 'small voice within'.

Try to listen very closely for that 'still, small voice' of inspiration, especially during meditation.

When you are able to sit quietly and open your mind, you connect in a way to an eternal library of knowledge.

All of the answers, to all of the questions you have, and all the methods to quickly take you from the life you live now, to the life you want to live in the near future, are there for the taking. All you have to do is relax, empty your thoughts, and allow these ideas, these answers to questions, these responses to the visualizations and affirmations you have been giving out, to drift into your mind.

Like a breath of fresh air, if you are open to the idea, the inspiration will come. Indeed the word itself comes from the Latin root, which is 'inspirare', meaning 'to be divinely breathed into'.

If you begin to sit quietly or meditate each day, forming clear pictures in your mind, using sights, sounds, smells, touch, taste and above all else, *feelings* for the life you desire, you *will* experience those inspirational moments. You will witness those 'coincidences' and hear that little voice of guidance in your head.

Observe them!

Let me give you an analogy. Imagine, if you will, a small battery-powered music player. The headphones are plugged in, the track is playing, and the volume is turned up loud. However, there's a problem. You're not wearing the headphones, so you can't hear anything! Furthermore, the music player is across the room, you're watching TV, and the volume is turned up loud to drown out the sound of the washing machine in the room next door, which is on its spin cycle right now.

Noise, noise, noise.

In my analogy, the washing machine represents the background noise of phones, billboards, newspaper headlines, social media, emails, and all the distractions of our 21st century life.

The blaring TV represents the constant noise in our heads. "Did I lock the back door?" "What should I have for dinner this evening?" "She looks fat." "He looks handsome." And so on.

The little music player is the still small voice of inspiration, linked directly to Source, calling out in its own delicate way, unnoticed.

That's how 95% of the Western world lives. Most people live out their lives completely oblivious to that still, small voice telling them exactly what to do in order to move towards their dream destination.

When we enter our quiet time, even for just ten minutes a day, we are turning off that washing machine.

When we slowly concentrate on our breathing and drift into meditation, we are holding out the remote and slowly turning down the TV, until it's on 'mute'.

As we allow thoughts to just drift by without judgement until our minds are quiet and still, we hear a distant sound. The music player across the room is making a sound. As our ears hone in on the whisper, we can make out the sound.

If we put on the headphones, we can be inspired by what we hear. It's not always a 'voice'; it can be a thought, spoken in my own voice inside my head, or it might be an image, or a memory that triggers an idea.

As I've said previously, you don't have to sit with your legs crossed, burning incense in a room full of candles to do this. You *will* receive inspiration while meditating, but you might also receive it during a long solo walk early in the morning. I daydream a lot as I trudge through the local woodland; sometimes a great idea pops into my head, usually related to something I've added to my vision board recently, or a new goal I've noted down. The same happens on a long drive.

Regardless of how, where, when and why, write them down. I started with a pen and notepad I carried everywhere with me. (Maybe not whilst driving—after a near-death experience on the motorway to London one day, I switched to a digital Dictaphone!) Start recording these little thoughts and feelings, ideas and inspirations. The more you capture, the more that arrive.

It's a fantastic feeling to receive so much feedback. As you work on your hopes and aspirations for the future, as you apply the ideas that come to you and see them work at bringing you closer to your dream, the whole world begins to open up before you.

Your easy challenge is to simply observe, to watch for the inspirations, instincts and coincidences that occur over the next few days.

Before you know it, you too will find yourself smiling at the situations you're creating for yourself.

Here are some examples from my life: "Why am I going to climb up onto a narrow ledge, pretend to get shot, and then dive head first towards the ground?" and "Why am I hidden inside a magic box on a stage, wearing handcuffs and tied inside a silk sack?!"

When you live your life on purpose, when you realize that any thought you can sustain in your mind can become reality, you have these thoughts quite often!

What about these: "Why am I climbing out of a hot air balloon approaching 30,000 feet above the ground, wearing an oxygen mask, where it's so cold that my breath is freezing as I breathe out, forming icicles on my chin?" and "Why are these people pasting flammable gum to my body, ready to set me on fire from head to foot in a few seconds? I must be nuts!"

Why, why, why indeed!

Because expanding our horizons is what life is all about. Living and experiencing everything there is to live and experience.

Overcoming obstacles is an extremely worthy experience. Doing things that are extremely challenging forces you to grow as an individual. The examples from my life might seem extreme, but we all have our own challenges, which are just as overwhelming if we look at them like that.

So observe, watch, listen, and notice the coincidences. Notice noticing the coincidences.

I'm sure if you looked closely enough at some key turning points in your life, you would recall some coincidences that led you there, or caused that change to occur.

One word of warning before I close this chapter.

Whenever you move from your 'current life' into the 'next stage' of your life, be it a new relationship, job, car, home or whatever, you're going to have a wobble!

When you improve your life, you raise your vibration. However, your subconscious mind is quite happy where it was, so it wants to pull you back down to where it's been for all this time.

The easiest thing to do, practised by tens of thousands of people every day, is to go back to what you were doing before. It's wonderful: you feel relaxed, you feel safe, your heart beats normally again, and you talk yourself out of your dream.

The other option, the one I prefer to choose, is to recognize I am in 'wobble territory', and know that this is a clear indicator that I am close to my goal.

I spend a lot of my life in this mode, and have come to get a perverse kick out of the uneasy feeling that accompanies change.

Stick with it. Holding the image of your dream in your conscious mind for long enough, around 30 days, allows the subconscious to erase the old mentality, and accept the new mind set.

The wisdom that Pierce revealed to me on that mountain, changed my life forever. It will change yours too, if you let it.

CHAPTER SIX

"He who has begun is half done."

— QUINTUS HORATIUS FLACCUS [HORACE] *(65BC – 8BC)*

Action

In disbelief I watched the sunlight trickle in through the cracks in the shuttered windows and ooze under the wooden door. Could it really be morning already?

I'd tossed and turned through the night, the same dream returning to me again and again, no matter what I did to block it.

A knock on the door.

"Hello?" I said, clearing my throat. "Hello?"

The door opened as the familiar gentle tones of Pierce's voice filled the room.

"Good morning, good morning. And how are we today? Suitably rested, I hope?"

"Well, not really. I had a bit of a restless night."

"Really?" he said, sitting at the foot of my bed. "Was it the cold? It can get extremely bitter this time of year up here."

"No, no. I just had a weird dream, one of those that I couldn't shake. I can still remember it, which is odd, as I usually forget my dreams when I wake up."

"You know, dreams are another way that we can receive inspiration. Thomas Edison used to take 'catnaps' several times a day, especially when he came upon a challenge in his inventing. He would consider the problem, and then take a short sleep, reporting that the solution often came to him while he slept."

"Really? I didn't know that."

"Yes. Many a famous inventor, scientist, writer, teacher, philosopher, film director and songwriter has acknowledged divine inspiration during sleep."

"My dream was weird though," I replied. "A bit too cryptic to mean anything, I think."

"Perhaps," came the reply. "But why not let me be the judge of that? Come, let us grab some hot gruel and be away from this place. The mountain beckons. You can tell me all about your dream as we climb."

All at Sea

We left the blue temple behind us and slowly spiralled up to the ridge we'd conquered the day before. This time, we walked its rocky spine towards the imposing tower, its head hidden beneath a veil of fine cloud.

The sky was clear, the air cold and crisp, as we crunched through the frozen snow.

"So tell me," Pierce began, as he slowed to allow me to walk beside him, "how did this dream begin?"

"It started in the sky, high above the sea. I was dressed as a pirate captain, floating above the clouds, looking down on a group of islands that formed the letter 'V'. There were fourteen in all; I counted them, seven forming the left side of the 'V' and seven forming the right side of the 'V'.

"Right at the bottom or point of the 'V' was a fine sailing ship, the sort you would see in a pirate movie. It had dropped anchor and was waiting for me, the ship's captain, to decide which way we were heading next."

I stopped for a second, borrowing Pierce's stick to scratch a diagram in the snow. I marked the position of the ship with an X and then drew circles to represent the islands.

"Now," I continued, slowly walking along the snowy ridge, "in this dream, the crew asked me, because I could fly, to go check out the islands. So I rose off the deck like Peter Pan, looked to the string of islands to the left, and flew off in the direction of the first island.

"The first was no more than a sandbank with a few windswept palm trees on it. It was called something like Dead Man's Isle. The next one was worse, fewer trees and very open to the elements. The next, Scorpion Island, was very rocky and exposed.

"The further I flew north, away from the ship, the worse the weather got. The constant wind from the east, blowing from my right-hand side as I tried to fly north, was getting stronger and stronger. By the time I reached the final island, the top left of the 'V' formation, I was being soaked by driving rain and buffeted violently by gusting winds while thunder and lightning echoed and danced around the surrounding sky. The volcano on the island was spewing lava out into the ocean, and the sulphurous odour in the air took my breath away. There could be no life on this island.

"I turned around and headed back to the ship, flying over the seven islands on my way back as the weather slowly improved. Safely back on the ship, I relayed to the crew that there was no point in heading to the islands on the left, for all of them were bad, and the further away you went, the worse they became. There was nothing for us to the left.

"The crew murmured—the sea currents were strong here, and came from the east. They knew that even if we headed right, without skilful sailing the ship would naturally drift to the left and be shipwrecked on one of the islands. The crew asked me to scout the other string of islands to the right.

"I floated into the air again, leaned forward and sped away towards the first island to our right. It was similar to the first on the other side, only its few palm trees were full of fruit. It looked like a good place to stop for a while. The next was similar, but had a few waterfalls—fresh water.

"As I flew onward, the weather improved, the wind lessened and the sun shone brightly. In a reversal of my previous flight, each island to the right kept getting better and better.

"I finally flew over Paradise Island to reach the seventh island, Heavenly Isle, which was populated with happy and prosperous people, who lived in perfect harmony. The trees were packed with all kinds of fruit, streams and waterfalls flowed abundantly, and the sound of peaceful laughter filled the air.

"I wanted to stay there, but in the dream I was dragged back to the ship, the weather deteriorating on the way back until I rejoined the crew on the overcast deck. I explained to them that we would hop from island to island, due northeast, and that each island would get better and better. With great excitement, we lifted anchor and set sail. That's when the dream got really irritating, Pierce."

"Really?" he replied, as we approached the peak and began to head upwards on the icy path. "In what way?"

"Well, no matter what we did, it was always a struggle to stay on the islands to the right because of the currents. Sometimes we'd make the first island, lift the sail, and then slowly drift west towards the first island on the bad side. The weather would worsen, the wind would pick up and eventually we'd be back where we started, at the bottom of the 'V' formation.

"Next, we'd reach the second or third island. I'd be enjoying the dream, and then suddenly, when I wasn't concentrating, the ship would lunge to the left and we'd scramble to save her, only to be carried west again to the second or third terrible island.

"The worse part in this annoying dream that went on all night, was the fact that the current was too strong to just turn around and head back. So if we reached the fourth island right of the 'V' formation, the current dragged us west to shipwreck on the fourth terrible island. The only way back would be to navigate south along the left side to the bottom of the 'V' to start all over again.

"I tossed and turned all night, Pierce, as we tried again and again to reach Heavenly Isle. Each time we'd get closer but the strong current from Heavenly Isle had its price. We'd almost run aground at the volcanic island, get soaked in the rain, choke on the fumes, and risk death from the lightning!

"Again we would have to head south, down the line of islands until we were once again at the starting point."

"And did you reach this nirvana-like island on the good side?" Pierce smiled as he raised his white eyebrow.

"No, not in the ship at least. We were drawing nearer for about the tenth time, when the sun rose and you came knocking at my door!"

Wind and Hot Tea

The talking stopped as we turned a corner on the spiral path and walked into a strong chilling wind. Pierce pulled his scarf up over his nose and mouth, and pulled down his woollen hat so only a thin slit remained for him to look through. I wore a 'tube', which is a versatile bit of headgear that can be a scarf, or a hat, or, in this case, a balaclava. A quick adjustment meant, like Pierce, I was walking head down into wind with only a thin slit to look through.

On we plodded, putting one foot in front of the other, as the path took us higher and higher, on a gradual spiral to the left. The terrain was rough going, large boulders blocking the way from time to time; sometimes snowdrifts had to be navigated, other times sheets of ice would make it difficult to negotiate and dangerously sharp if we stumbled.

We eventually turned side-on to the wind, reaching a section where the freezing gusts were behind us. Here we spotted a large boulder, some 30 feet high. As soon as I got around the rock, I felt instant warmth. It wasn't the air temperature, but the relief of getting out of the wind chill.

Out came my small flask, for the best cup of tea I'd ever had.

"So," I said to Pierce, "this dream of mine."

"Oh," he replied, "the ramblings of a mad man. It clearly means nothing."

I looked up from my steaming cup of tea, for signs of Pierce joking. He looked very serious, and then broke into a smile.

"I am pulling your leg, of course," he said. "I am jesting." Pierce glanced skyward, his face taking on the character of a head teacher about to address the school assembly. "Your dream seems quite obvious to me. Especially when you consider what we have been speaking of these past few days—your ability to create whatever life you choose for yourself—the imagery becomes clear."

"Go on," I said, removing my gloves for a moment to feel the warmth of the hot cup against my hands.

"Well, in life, we always want to better ourselves, to improve our lot. In your dream, this could be likened to sailing towards the good islands, starting with the first one with the fruit on it. Ultimately, we all want to get to that Heavenly Isle—everything we could ever want and need.

"However, we cannot just arrive suddenly at this island one day. We must start with the very idea in our mind of visiting Heavenly Isle. We need to imagine our arrival, and do so mentally every day. Then we take out our map and plan our journey.

"Any seafarer worth their salt would know that the only way to reach the seventh island safely would be to navigate to the first island, and perhaps rest and stock up with fruit and water.

"So that is what we do in real life, as in your dream. Take action, the first few steps in the direction of your desires.

"Once rested, we would set course for the second island. Upon arrival we would stock up on food and drink, and check out the ship's rigging, sails and rudder. And so it would continue: planning the route from one island to the next, taking action to correct our steering as the winds and currents try to blow us off course to the west, where the poor weather and terrible islands of frustration and despair await us.

"Eventually, with practised thought, planning and plenty of action, we would arrive at our ultimate destination and bathe in the glory of our abundant lives."

"I like that," I smiled, "but I think there was more going on; the ship would drift west to the bad islands if we relaxed for more than a moment."

"Correct!" beamed Pierce. "In your dream, had you sat on the deck of the ship with the anchor down, twiddling your thumbs, you would never have reached the first island, let alone the seventh island! You had to bring up the anchor, having planned the course, and set the rudder accordingly. You had to make adjustments, like lowering the sail, before you even started moving towards your goal.

"Daily action is essential. I would go so far as to say 'massive action' is essential if you wish to live the life you were truly born to live.

"It saddens me that so many people lose sight of this simple fact. They take their focus away from their dream, distracted by some unimportant thing. This might be likened to letting go of the ship's rudder in your dream. Life, like the sea currents you mentioned, simply takes them away from their goals, and before they know it, they can be in murky waters.

"The current could be likened to the masses of people who get up each day, eat the same breakfast, take the same route to work in the same job, return back by the same route, watch TV, then go to bed and get up the next day to do it all again!

"The current—the consciousness of the masses—does not flow towards creation but forces competition.

"When we stop dreaming, stop believing, stop setting goals and stop taking daily action, we drift away from the beautiful islands we are meant to inhabit. We need to make a conscious effort, daily, to focus on our maps and man the ship's wheel, while all the time watching out for obstacles that might impede our progress."

"Wow, I get it!" I said with a broad smile. "You're so insightful, Pierce. I rarely dream so clearly, and certainly don't remember having had any dream like that before."

"That will be the altitude," Pierce replied, as he prepared to leave the shelter of the rock and continue up the mountain. "They say the pure rarefied air encourages great sleep and wonderful dreams."

We stepped out from our shelter into a freezing wind that pushed us forwards from behind. Forwards and upwards towards the prize that awaited only the toughest and persistent of adventurers.

Mind the Gap

"Stay back!" shouted Pierce from a steep snowy bank ahead.

"What's wrong?" I shouted back up the slope, stopping in my tracks.

He didn't answer. Instead he turned and went back over the crest of the hill, out of sight. Moments later, he re-emerged and slid back down the snowy bank.

"It is not good, my friend. The bridge is out."

"The bridge is out? What does that mean? We have to go a different way?"

"Perhaps not. You work in the movies as a performer of stunts, do you not?"

I nodded curiously.

"Then come. Let me know how you feel about making this crossing."

We ascended the slippery slope and at the top, with a strong wind thrashing around us, he pointed to a sheer rock face.

A narrow path, only two feet in width, hugged the rock face. However, from where we were standing, we could not get to that path because there was a gap. Several feet to my right, I could see some old worn ropes spanning the gap, but no bridge. Old bits of wood littered the edges of the cliff on either side.

I moved forward for a closer look.

"Be careful," said Pierce. "Do not get too close in this wind."

The gap was greater than I'd first thought, about seven feet wide. As I neared the edge, my heart leapt into my throat. I couldn't see the bottom it was so far beneath me.

I shuddered, and walked backwards away from the edge.

Had the seven-foot gap been at ground level, perhaps a seven-foot wide stream, I'd have had no problem taking a run at it and jumping. With the gap a thousand feet or more in the air, my perception changed.

The weather was unusual, still bright and sunny, yet the winds were unpredictable. Occasionally they would rest, sometimes just a breeze, then from nowhere they would gust with the strength of a hurricane to blow you sideways and onto your knees.

"I guess we should backtrack and find an alternative route," I shouted to Pierce, above the noise of the whistling wind.

"You may be correct."

"I am. We have no ropes to tie ourselves off in the event of a slip," I replied.

"Unless," Pierce said, pointing to our left, "we can use that?"

He motioned to what looked like a stretcher—a few long lengths of rough wood, about ten feet in length, tied together. Clearly someone had either started to make a new bridge, or this was an aborted attempt. The contraption looked quite weathered.

I decided to place the boards across the gap, and then to make a decision, although without ropes and harnesses I wasn't keen. Still, I'd come this far, and the gap was only seven feet, after all. The boards were heavy, but the smooth frozen ground beneath helped me to slide them to the edge, and with a focussed burst of energy, I managed to shove the boards across the gap.

We had an extremely makeshift method of crossing the expanse.

As I waited, dry throated, for the wind to settle, I glanced over to the other side and spotted an old climbing rope in the distance, almost around the corner where the narrow path turned out of view around the cliff face. It looked long enough to throw across the gap as a safety line.

I made my decision. "Pierce, I'm going to keep low and move quickly across the wood to the other side."

"All right, I will follow if you think it safe."

"No. There's a rope. Let me cross, and then I'll run over and get the rope, come back, secure one end over there, and throw it to you."

"Good thinking. I will keep the wood steady while you go and get the rope then. Be very careful. Please."

To be honest with you, I was really scared.

However, it seemed the right thing to do. Pierce had led from the front all of the way up the mountain so far, and here I had the opportunity to help out Pierce for a change.

Gently Does It

Pierce crouched to support the wooden planks, and with one last breath I stepped out onto the makeshift bridge.

The moment I did so, the boards began to sag and creak. My heart was in my mouth. A slow step, followed by a quicker one, followed by a hop and a jump, and I was across!

"OK," I said. "Wait there."

I ran to fetch the rope, trying not to look down to my left at the very high drop that would greet me if I were to trip. By the time I'd reached the end of the rope and coiled it in, I had turned around the bend in the cliff face, out of Pierce's view.

"Almost done!" I shouted to Pierce. *"Back in a second!"*

Just then a strong wind slammed the left side of my body into the hard wall of rock. I dropped quickly to avoid being blown off the edge.

"Hang in there, Pierce!" I shouted. *"I've got the rope."*

The wind died down, and I carefully edged back around the corner to greet my friend and mentor.

When I arrived, I recoiled in horror. The wooden planks were gone. And so was Pierce.

"Pierce!" I yelled at the top of my voice, giving no thought to the avalanche that might answer my scream of desperation.

Where was the bridge? Where was Pierce? What was happening? I wanted to jump back across the gap to look for him, but now had no space to run from.

"Pierce! Pierce!" I yelled again, my voice barely audible over the wind.

The monumental impact of what had happened hit me and I dropped to my knees, this time in shock and desperation.

Pierce had gone.

Had the wind picked up the planks of wood as he held them, and dragged him to his death? Or had Pierce grown concerned about how long I had been gone, and been crossing the bridge when the gust came along? Was it my fault?

It was then that I realized just how attached to Pierce I had become. Sometimes in life it is only when we lose something that we realize the true value of that thing we took for granted.

I cried that day on the mountain for the first time in 25 years. I *really* cried. I sobbed my heart out like the little boy I once was, only there was nobody there to cradle me and wipe away my tears.

I was alone.

So utterly alone.

Through Teary Eyes

I have no idea how long I knelt on the ledge that day, looking down into the chasm. It felt like many hours, but was probably minutes.

The wind was growing stronger, and I suddenly became aware of how very cold I was. The mountain had taken one life today, and was not going to take another. Following the natural curve of the rock face once more, I retraced my footsteps around the corner to where I'd grabbed the rope, and continued. The path widened into a gentle descent.

Only one lone peak remained ahead, the mountain summit, glowing in the midday sun.

"Should I try for the summit?" I thought. "Only one day away if I knew the route."

I then scolded myself for even considering it. My only task now was to find the temple—not only a bed for the night, but a place to plan my descent from the mountain and the recovery of my friend's body.

Looking down from my vantage point, I spotted what looked like a winding path that widened as it descended.

Like a young child separated from its parent, tears streaming down my face, I trundled lonely and confused down the rocky path.

With each plodding step, I tortured myself: "Why did I leave him to go for the rope?... Why didn't he stay put?... Had I not left him, I could have stopped him crossing."

Occasionally the path would take me upwards again, circling the final peak that housed the summit I'd sought for so long. Just when I began to doubt my route, the path would steeply descend once more. Each time it did, the wind would lessen and the temperature rise.

I must have walked for around three hours that day, before noticing I was tired physically and exhausted mentally. I stopped for a moment, my legs shaking from exertion. The sweat trickled down my brow into my eyebrows, and then on into my squinting eyes.

Suddenly I felt like I was being watched.

In the back of beyond, close to the end of my tether, I sensed that above and behind me, I was being studied. I spun my head to the right and staggered backwards in awe.

Refuge

A beautiful lone building looked out from the top of the hill, surveying the valley below with her watchful eye. She shone like a piece of purple amethyst on a bed of frozen grey slate.

With renewed energy, I turned on my heels and darted towards her, slipping and sliding. I jogged up the frozen scree to the top of the hill and arrived with gritted teeth on a carefully laid stone path—the path that led to the finest temple I had ever seen.

Tears welled up in my eyes, whether tears of relief at having found shelter or tears of guilt and regret for the loss of my friend, or perhaps a mixture of both.

I wiped my eyes and nose, and began to compose myself as I slowly walked the level path to the temple.

No village here, I noted, just a stone path to a lilac temple – like Dorothy's yellow brick road to the gates of the Emerald City.

Three straight, smooth pillars guarded the entrance. Beautiful amethyst colours danced like shadow puppets upon the walls, light reflected from small pools of water that surrounded the temple. The beauty took my breath away.

At the door a familiar sweet aroma filled the air. Until this point, the fragrances had been generic herbs and spices drifting on a breeze, or in-distinguishable odours from combined incense sticks and cones. Here, though, was the familiar scent of lavender oil, which I used at home on burns and to aid restful sleep. Indeed my children often drifted to sleep with the scent of lavender on their pillows. It seemed somehow out of place in this part of the world, a plant I associated more with the lavender fields of North Yorkshire than this inhospitable terrain at the top of the world.

A sudden feeling of calm overcame me as I reached for a white tas-selled cord that hung down in front of the purple entrance doors. I gen-tly pulled the soft rope and heard the high tinkle of small bells, which sounded more like wind chimes than the circular heavy bell I expected.

With the twinkling chorus still adrift on the cool mountain breeze, the doors rocked and began to swing inwards. As they did so, they opened my eyes to a glorious sight.

I understood at once why there was no village around the temple — the villagers lived inside! Dozens and dozens of them went about their daily business in a calm and efficient manner. Every one of them who caught my eye, bowed and smiled warmly. The people here seemed very happy.

An elderly gentleman emerged from behind the door. "My friend, you are most welcome."

The man, clothed in the finest purple robes, gently placed his left hand in the small of my back, to lead me into the courtyard in front of me.

"You stay and rest, my friend? You must be most hungry, and in need of much sleep?"

"I am tired," I replied, "and I do need to rest, but there was an accident earlier and I need to..."

"Slow down, please, relax," said the temple worker, as I realized I was talking loudly, my emotions bubbling to the surface.

"Please," he said, pointing to a lilac door at the end of an alleyway, "feel free to wash and rest a moment, then we shall talk."

I respected his request and left him as I walked between two whitewashed buildings, pausing for a moment at the lilac door. Wondering what the astronomical symbols on the door could mean, I turned the silver door handle to enter my room for the evening. As the door swung open, my jaw dropped, and every ounce of air left my lungs.

The Unexpected Visitor

"What kept you?" came the slow, familiar voice that had gently assisted me up the mountain. Pierce!

He was sitting at the foot of a fine bed. He smiled broadly and stood as he placed his hands on his hips.

I tried to speak, but was fighting back tears of relief. "I thought you were..."

"Narrow escape, my young friend, a very narrow escape."

"But how did you...?"

"I did not fall as far as you might imagine, and with deep snow on a ledge below, no harm has been done. I am fine."

I started to laugh uncontrollably, pure relief. Pierce soon joined me, probably quite relieved himself.

"Your face!" he laughed. "I have never seen a person's mouth open quite so wide as yours!"

"Pierce, I'm so happy to be the source of your amusement again, I really am. I thought I'd lost you!"

The smile slowly dropped from Pierce's face as he at first looked serious, and then a little sad. "No, my dear friend. You have not lost me. I am here for you."

With that, he took a sharp intake of breath, clapped his wrinkled hands and forced a smile.

"Come!" he said. "How did you find climbing alone? How did you find this place?"

I went over the events surrounding the accident and tried my best to explain my shock, and the feeling of helplessness that followed. Pierce nodded a lot. He reminded me that everything happens for a reason and that I had learned several lessons that day.

One lesson was how I'd assumed Pierce would always be there, to lead me up to the summit, and all the way down again. I had, in a way, taken that for granted. It was only when he was gone that I realized how much I needed him. He had become a good friend, and yet I hadn't thanked him enough for all his wise words and help.

I learned then the danger of putting things off. From that day forth I would always take action that day, rather than when I got around to it.

Another lesson that I'd learned, was that Pierce was correct: I was able to hear that still, small voice, and follow my instincts.

The purple temple had been above and behind me, yet for some reason, I had had that sense of someone watching me. By being forced to walk alone for hours in silence, I'd fine-tuned that ability and found the temple. Had I not done so, I could have easily perished, lost on the mountain.

I rejoiced at having found the temple. "I was amazed to find it more like a little walled village above the clouds. And the people, they seem very happy and content."

"Yes," Pierce replied. "They are a most hospitable bunch, and always have been. I was one of the first white men to visit this place, but that was a long, long time ago. Did you know that legend says a tall bearded white man helped design a lot of the temples on this mountain? I heard that a similar story is told in South America, about a bearded white wise man pre-dating the Incas and Mayans!

"For all the many years I have known these people, they have been positive people. They are serene, and walk around with a definite air of optimism and purpose. They live in faith, and they believe that their thoughts create things, and that they can connect to a divine intelligence for guidance and inspiration.

"Better still, they are busy people, taking action daily. They are not work shy; this beautiful walled sacred village is a testament to that."

"Amazing," I said. "I love it here."

"Indeed, so do I. Shall we rest a while? You look very tired, and we have both had a strenuous and testing day. You go ahead and slip off your boots to lie down. I shall speak with the elders and then do exactly the same."

Pierce made for the door, and as he began to open it, I called, "Pierce!"

"Yes?"

"It's great to have you here," I said in a whisper.

"It is great to be here with you, my friend. The pleasure is all mine."

He smiled, bowed his head slightly, and left the room, gently closing the door behind him.

I eased back onto my luxurious bed in a state of blissful relaxation. It was by far the largest bed I'd used on the mountain so far, close to the size of a double bed in the West, and piled with heavy purple blankets that gave the bed a 'royal' feel.

My legs felt remarkably good considering the number of miles covered that day. Only my difficulty in fully breathing remained, otherwise I felt fantastic. I placed my hands behind my head to relax.

Thoughts turned to the events of that day, from the chat about my dream and what it might have meant, to the talk of taking action, on a colossal scale. From confronting my fear as I crossed the dangerous chasm, to the heartfelt loss on thinking Pierce had fallen to his death. Then the utter relief and immense gratitude of finding him waiting for me at the temple, and the temple itself; nothing could have prepared me for its beauty and the wonderful feeling of satisfaction within its walls.

The dream, taking action, reaching a high altitude, facing fears, relief and gratitude, followed by an intense feeling of satisfaction.

I could have been describing the story of my first Guinness World Record attempt.

| High Flying |

I had wanted to jump from a great height for as long as I could remember. I watched TV shows that featured parachuting with wide-eyed excitement. The opening title sequence of my favourite childhood TV show *The Fall Guy* comes to mind.

The brilliant Lee Majors first captured my attention in the seventies as Steve Austin in *The Six Million Dollar Man*; he was my hero. Soon after that series ended, Lee Majors managed to quickly reinvent himself as Hollywood stuntman Colt Seavers in the hit TV show *The Fall Guy*. It first aired in the UK in 1981 when I was 11 years old. One episode, and I was hooked.

I recall the opening sequence, a compilation of classic stunts that we are supposed to believe Colt Seavers performed. For one of them, a bit of clever editing makes it look like Lee Majors himself jumps head first from a small aircraft. For some reason, Colt Seavers diving head first from an aircraft stayed with me, as did my ambition to become a Hollywood stuntman.

Within three years, at the age of 14, I'd written a letter enquiring about parachute clubs to my local Citizens Advice Bureau. This was a magical place to me, an office in Middlesbrough that I could write to, enclosing a stamped addressed envelope, and ask any question. As if consulting the great Oracle of Delphi, I began writing to the Citizens Advice Bureau at the age of ten. It seemed quite natural back then to post letters and postcards to TV shows and kids' magazines, so writing to the bureau seemed a normal pastime.

I now wonder what they made of me, a ten-year-old trying to find out how to become a stuntman! Credit where it's due, they took my request seriously and answered me each and every time. For the 'How do I become a stuntman?' question, they told me to write to the actors' union, and gave me their address. I wrote to the actors' union, Equity, and was given a list of skills that I'd need if I were to become a stuntman one day, a list I would eventually retrieve and use as a blueprint to my success.

So it was, that as a 14-year-old boy, I received a reply from the Citizens Advice Bureau regarding my skydiving enquiry. They kindly put me in touch with the Cleveland Parachute Club. Imagine my excitement when a lady called Brenda wrote back, to tell me that the club were parachuting into my town in a fortnight! I got to Albert Park just in time to see them spiralling in with smoke canisters billowing from their ankles. I was a shy boy, but it was 1984 and having completed a half-marathon that year, I had new-found confidence. I approached the jumpers to find Brenda.

She chatted to me about my ambitions to parachute, but I mainly stood in awe of her. I looked at her jumpsuit and thought, "Wow, a few minutes ago, that jumpsuit was hurtling through the sky at 120 miles per hour!"

I was going to become a stuntman, and one of the six required skills I would master would be parachuting. I signed up at 16 years of age, and after a few faltering starts due to poor weather, did my first jump when I was 17, in 1987.

I'd leapt from an aeroplane flying 2,000 feet above the ground and lived to tell the tale. I was hooked! One down, and only another 49 jumps to go before I had my first stunt qualification. Had I known the rules would later require a further 199 jumps, I might have reconsidered.

The mixture of adverse weather, lack of funds, having no transport and the fact that the club was only open at weekends meant progress was slow.

My goal was a level of achievement called the Category 8, or 'Cat 8'—one of the six stunt qualifications I needed to become a stuntman. I needed to be Cat 8 and to have performed 50 parachute jumps.

Following your first static line jump at 2,000 feet you were Cat 1, and by the time you were Cat 8 you'd be able to dive head first out of an aircraft at 10,000 feet, spin a couple of times left and right, always stopping on the same heading, do a back somersault, then read your altitude from a meter on your chest, turn 180 degrees, put your arms by your sides to accelerate away, and deploy your parachute by 2,000 feet.

I got my Cat 8 'wings' in August of 1990.

I wanted to jump higher, but the limit was 10,000 feet.

By then, I'd had a fantastic time learning to skydive and achieved my first stunt qualification, but as I couldn't jump higher I would save parachuting for the occasional 'fun jump' on a sunny day. Besides, I was close to being a black belt in Judo, ready to take my swimming tests, teaching fencing at Teesside University, still horse riding a few times a week, and now trampolining and springboard diving too.

For the next six years, as I completed my stunt training, moved to Nottingham, got my Equity Card and started doing acting on the stage and TV, I only jumped out of an aeroplane 12 times.

Go West, Where the Skies Are Blue

It was a friend from the medieval banquet I was still performing at who brought me out of skydiving retirement. Scotty had decided to pursue a career as a stuntman too, his imagination captured by my stories of skydiving, hang gliding, scuba diving, and the like.

One day he told me that the skydiving requirements for the British Stunt Register had changed. It was no longer a mere Category 8 qualification, he explained, but had moved to Cat 10—the highest possible skill level attainable!

Things had moved on a lot since my skydiving training some six years previous—new canopies, much faster progression through the Categories, fancy safety devices. My friend needed to learn to skydive, and to do so quickly. I needed to blow the dust from my jumpsuit and move from Cat 8 to Cat 10 as quickly as possible.

There was only one place to do this—America. The only snag was neither of us had any money, and neither us had flown abroad before.

That did not stop us. Naturally, everything came together.

We flew to New York, because the tickets were cheaper than flying to Florida where the skydiving was. As the plane descended, I was apprehensive—I had never landed in an aircraft before, despite taking off on 62 other occasions! Then we caught a Greyhound bus all the way down to Florida, where we arrived after 36 hours in the same seat and having covered another 1,200 miles.

What followed was as far away from British skydiving as could possibly be imagined.

There certainly wasn't any waiting around at the Lake Wales Skydiving Centre. Every day was a skydiving day, from the moment you opened your eyes to the final lift taking off in near darkness for those memorable 'sunset jumps'.

The freedom of hurtling head-low over the Florida swamps at 180 miles per hour, wearing only shorts and a T-shirt, was exhilarating.

What would have taken me another year of dedicated weekend parachuting in the UK took me a little over five days; it was over in just 12 jumps from 16,000 feet.

What followed was a grand American adventure, driving with Scotty across the entire United States from east to west. We finally arrived in Hollywood, only to drive into the middle of some kind of 'gang culture' competition; there we were pulled over and nearly arrested by a gun-wielding cop. From there we visited San Clemente, San Diego, popped into Universal Studios back in Hollywood, and then headed north to San Francisco, where we spent a few days with Scotty's relatives.

My tired friend flew back to the UK, and I flew out to Ireland—an acting job had manifested right before our departure that would pay for the parachuting.

From Dublin I flew right back to the States on my own, for several more weeks of touring and visiting friends. I still had that return flight from New York in my pocket, and was determined to use it!

| Ever Higher |

My first expedition across America changed me, as only travel can. Like my expedition across Europe from England to the Black Sea only four years previous, it expanded my mind and reinforced the fact that anything is possible—the goals, the daily visualizations, the daily action, often huge action, with no apparent way to finance the trip.

What a journey my skydiving had taken me on! From those starry-eyed letters as a 14-year-old, to my first faltering steps to the parachute centre as a 16-year-old, from my first jump at 17, through all of those memorable weekends that led me to both the end of my teens, and my 'parachuting wings'.

And then, America, and what I thought would be the end of my parachuting adventures. I'd gone from terrifying static line jumps from 2,000 feet to acrobatic skydives from 16,000 feet. I still wanted to go higher, of course, but the limit in the UK was 12,000 feet on a good day.

So it seemed I would have to accept that I would never parachute any higher. Unless of course I could blag some high altitude oxygen kit and hitch a ride on a high flying hot-air balloon. But that could never happen.

Could it?

I'd dreamed of 'jumping high' for many years. I recall watching a British TV show called *Q.E.D.* while I was still learning to skydive in my teens. It followed the exploits of two men aiming to break the British Record for Highest Parachute Jump. The show started with business-man Rory McCarthy, explaining why he chose that particular record, and ended with famous balloonist Per Lindstrand taking McCarthy and his friend up to 39,000 feet, where they successfully jumped into the British Record Books.

I kept that documentary on video cassette for over a decade, and watched it over and over.

I initially sought the help of the balloon pilot in that documentary, Per Lindstrand, when I was about 20 years old. Per very kindly wrote back to me, and agreed to build and fly the balloon for me if I raised the cash. I spent the next year writing to every company I could think of, seeking a sponsor, with no success.

Eventually, I was forced to press the pause button on the project. Not to worry. 'Pressing the pause button' is not the same as 'press-ing the stop button'. A 'pause button' can be un-pressed, and start the wheels in motion once more.

It was to be some 12 years later when I finally reactivated the project to parachute into the record books.

I had learned a lot since my late teens, and things had changed. In my late teens I was just another guy who wanted to be a stuntman, and doing a lot of training. As I turned 30 years old, I had become a profes-sional stuntman and had appeared in a James Bond movie—my claim to fame at the time.

And so it was, that after a lot of emailing, phone calls and faxes, I eventually got a very encouraging call from a guy called Jim Crosbie. Jim worked for a little-known company in West Yorkshire, called Damart Thermal Wear.

Another aspect that had changed since I first wrote to balloonist Per Lindstrand, was the record itself. Although what I'd witnessed in the Q.E.D. documentary was very impressive, it was a British Record, not a World Record. They had fallen something like 38,000 feet in freefall, but the Guinness World Record was more like 85,000 feet, established by Captain Joe Kittinger back in 1960.

I began to explore the possibilities of jumping high from the balloon, but instead of freefalling a long way, I would pull the parachute early, so that I was flying the canopy at that rarefied altitude. I checked with Guinness World Records and discovered a parachute had once stayed up back in the 1950s for a whole 40 minutes due to thermals rising from the ground.

A 40-minute parachute jump! That was some challenge.

I decided to go for that World Record instead. If I were going to attempt the freefall record, then I'd go after Joe Kittinger's record and jump from the edge of space. That would cost around £2 million—a larger project for another day.

Instead, I would fly in a balloon to 32,000 feet above the ground, jump out and deploy my parachute right away, and then try to fly it for longer than 40 minutes.

Having made that decision, and with Damart Thermal Wear interested in getting their logo on my parachute canopy, Operation Hawk was born.

| Operation Hawk |

Ten months later, I stood nervously on a tiny wooden step, looking down beyond my toes at the carpet of cloud many thousands of feet below.

Moments earlier I had glanced over at my balloon pilot, Charlie Limon. He was a new friend who had taken me to this great height to perform the world's longest ever parachute jump.

"*25,000 feet,*" he'd yelled. He was wearing a full face oxygen mask and helmet, the exhaust near his mouth frozen due to the extreme cold.

"Higher, Charlie!" I'd pleaded.

"I can't! Sorry, Curtis. I can't risk it. We're low on fuel and it's a long way down."

Charlie and I discussed whether or not to abort, but it had taken us many gruelling days to find the right conditions for take-off, driving from England through France and Spain into Portugal, with a disastrous detour to Morocco. What was designed as a three day mission had become a two week expedition covering five countries. At the edge of the Sierra Morena mountain range, and against all the odds, we had finally found our launch window in a place called Pozoblanco.

Scotty was with me again on his first expedition since our skydiving trip across America some six years previous. He played gooseberry to my long-suffering wife, who had come along to kiss her husband goodbye as the balloon launched.

It was 14 February 2002—Valentine's Day.

Ten months after finding a sponsor, and some 12 years after first visualizing myself parachuting into the record books from a high flying balloon, I was about to actually do it.

I had so much equipment strapped to me I could barely move—not only the large, cumbersome parachute and container, but a personal oxygen cylinder on my belly, recording equipment, battery packs with heated systems, cameras, timers, altimeters, transponder and even a GPS tracking device with spare batteries. I'd test jumped with various systems, but this was the first time I was to jump with *all* of the equipment together.

Too late to change my mind now!

I had spent so long organizing this record attempt, and so long trying to get the balloon airborne, that I'd stopped thinking about the jump itself, just the logistics behind it.

Although it had been less than a year, our hyperbaric training with the SAS, equipment tests in industrial freezer rooms and high altitude test jumps seemed a lifetime ago.

All of those long days, weeks and months of laser focussed dedication had led to this one moment.

Charlie looked between me and the large on-board clock that the cameras were filming. The second hand reached the 11 o'clock position as time suddenly slowed down to a slow motion crawl.

"And... ready... set... *go!*"

I dived up and out, arching my back so hard that I was looking upside down at Charlie for a beat, before he shot off above me. As he did so, a hard pull tore the parachute from my back, and threw me around like a rag doll for a moment as the canopy snapped open and spun me around for half a turn.

I quickly grabbed the toggles, pulled them down to flare the large square parachute, and then released them to feel the canopy surge forward.

I realized I was holding my breath, and nervously breathed out, not certain if my personal oxygen system would allow me to breathe back in after such a hard opening. It functioned perfectly, allowing me to breathe out, and the demand valve worked too, feeding me pure oxygen as I flew 25,000 feet above the earth.

Jump, okay. Parachute, okay. Oxygen systems, okay.

It was only minutes before the balloon caught me up, looming down from above like an eagle spreading its wings as it closed in on its prey. An amazing sight, as I watched Charlie's balloon fall below me. Like a moth to a lantern, I buzzed around the hot-air balloon, twice as high as civilian skydivers normally jump and 12 times higher than they normally fly a parachute!

And so we continued, staying close to one another as the air became thicker and warmer, and the ice began to melt and drip down on me from the parachute above.

We broke through the patchy cloud base at around 17,000 feet, revealing a sunlit expanse of Spanish mountains and sleeping vineyards far below.

A quick time check revealed that I'd descended faster than expected, possibly due to the increased weight of all the equipment, and the thin air.

The air heated quickly, so by 5,000 feet the flight began to get choppy, the warm thermals buffeting and almost collapsing the canopy. I reached up a few times to pull on the risers, to alter the shape of the parachute 'wing', and then went back to steering lines when it calmed down.

Suddenly Charlie lit both burners full blast, forcing the flames to billow hard and loud. The balloon lifted quickly above me. I lowered my eyes to my flight path and saw why he had ascended.

A large mountain lay ahead, covered in trees.

I checked my altitude—2,000 feet—and began to plan my landing.

The only challenge was, there was nowhere to land!

I'd descended over woodland, with little to no fields, and fewer flat areas. As 2,000 feet became 1,000 feet I noticed more and more hazards—valleys, rocky slopes, dense woodlands.

I was descending too quickly and had to prepare for an emergency landing. As I flew maybe 60 feet above the woods, I realized the edge of the treeline was actually a path, and turned slowly to line up with it.

No room for error. If I landed short or overshot my new target, I'd be in big trouble.

The ground rushed up to greet me. I flared my parachute but nothing happened. I hit the ground hard and bounced onto my right side, which knocked the wind out of me for a moment.

Before I allowed any pain to register, I quickly checked my wrist watch, just in time to see the second hand sweep towards the top of the clock face.

I'd flown for 44 minutes and 58 seconds, although we later realized that I'd jumped a couple of seconds early, and so the official flight time was 45 minutes.

I'd flown for five minutes more than the previous Guinness World Record!

Surprisingly, there was no immediate feeling of jubilation.

I was in the back of beyond in the searing heat, and had not seen the support vehicles anywhere. Still, nothing was broken. I gathered up and hid the parachute under a bush, and then rolled down my heavy flight suit. I began to walk. The 'path' I'd spotted from the air was actually a very narrow road, and rescue came in the form of a local car 30 minutes later.

Soon I was reunited with my support team and my tearful wife, who had feared the worst when communications had been lost with the balloon for several nerve-racking hours.

The big hug and kiss were followed by a huge cheer when I explained that for 45 of those nail-biting minutes, I'd flown my parachute into the record books.

I'd done it. I was a World Record breaker.

An Inspiring Banquet

After a long rest recalling my parachuting adventures, I rose fully recharged and ready to eat. By the time the temple worker knocked on my door, I'd already freshened up and changed my clothing for dinner.

I was made most welcome, and knelt to eat with the head man of the village at the top of the room. I wanted Pierce to join me, but he hung back in the shadows and let me enjoy the meal prepared in my honour.

They had varied questions about the Western world, mainly concerned with humanitarian issues rather than materialistic ones. Questions were passed down the line to me, translated, and the answers passed back down the line.

Chatter eventually drifted onto the subject of creating our own world using the power of our minds. To my surprise, they were all as knowledgeable as Pierce on the subject. I surmised that it was by visiting the temples that Pierce had gained his incredible knowledge. The head priest discussed the value of setting worthy aspirations, recording aims and desires, and taking regular action.

MASSIVE ACTION

You, reading this book, right here and now, have the ability to accept this wisdom that I am passing on to you. Doing so will change your life completely. But only if you execute each and every step. One of the most important is to take action: *initial action* and *sustained action.*

Initial action would be to decide to finish this book, sustained action would be to keep reading it.

After the book, initial action would be to set aside quiet time, to explore relaxation, to try meditation. Sustained action would be getting to bed 15 minutes earlier than usual, and setting your alarm clock 15 minutes earlier for the next morning. Then actually getting out of bed, rather than hitting the snooze button!

Once out of bed, you would perhaps have your morning drink to wake up a little, and then sit quietly, breathe slowly, concentrate on your breathing, and just sit and relax with an empty mind.

I'm only asking you to devote a minimum of ten minutes a day to sitting in silence and doing nothing—but to do so every day. The initial aim is to sit quietly for ten minutes each day, preferably in the morning when all is still and quiet.

As you relax into it, the ten minutes will become 15 minutes, then 20 minutes, until you are relaxing in bliss for 30 or even 40 minutes each morning. The ultimate goal would be to do this in the morning and at night.

The truth is, after just a few weeks of doing this, you will feel so much benefit that you will look forward to it. You'll start to experiment with different meditations, like the beach meditation I often do.

Within those meditations, once you're comfortable, you consider your goal. You might remember the images on your vision board, and then turn those into living images inside your head by bringing in the senses.

So if your goal is to own a gleaming white boat, and to sail it around the Mediterranean, you might remember the photo of the boat on your vision board, then you might see the vessel bobbing up and down in the water, and hear the splash of water as it butts against the jetty. The sea air might fill your nostrils as you feel the sun on your face, taste the salt in the air and hear the background noise of the seabirds circling overhead.

You would immerse yourself in the moment, then look skyward, or out to the horizon, and give thanks. Send out vibes of gratitude to the Universe: you are so happy and grateful to own this beautiful boat!

Whatever the goal, immerse yourself in it while meditating, give thanks, and then come back to your waking state, and feel wonderful. You can now go about your daily business in an excited way, knowing you are moving in the direction of your dreams and that your dreams are moving towards you, too.

You choose your future, and all the things you want in it. Think about those things every day as if you already have them. You think about them and give thanks for them in the present tense.

Then, take action.

Notice little coincidences that relate to the dream you are pursuing. Don't worry about *how* it will come about! The hints will keep arriving, the coincidences will stack up, until the penny finally drops and you take action.

Action is crucial.

Action is a link in the chain of creation; without it, we stand still and stagnate. The world is evolving all around us at a fantastic pace, so if you take no action, if you do nothing, you actually go backwards! You have to take some kind of action just to keep up with the evolution taking place in your world, which is why it takes *massive action* to slip into a higher gear and move away from the crowd.

Thoughts and feelings, sustained thoughts and feelings filter down from your limited conscious mind, into the powerful subconscious mind. Once there, they begin to work wonders. All that remains is for you to take action.

Then your thoughts really do become 'things'.

TWENTY-EIGHT DAYS

There is something especially powerful about taking action daily (without a break) for around 28 days.

I have learned that this has to do with the brain's method of creating neural pathways, which is what it does whenever we learn a new skill. If you break the daily habit for just one day, the whole 25 to 30 day process starts all over again.

This was brilliantly illustrated in an early NASA test, when a number of trainee astronauts were asked to wear special 'image inverting' glasses for 24 hours a day. The glasses had lenses in them that inverted the image they saw. The idea was to study the psychological effects of living with the tremendous stress and anxiety of an inverted world.

After about 28 days, something happened that caught the NASA scientists completely off guard.

One by one, each of the trainee astronauts woke up wearing the glasses to find they were looking at the world the right way up! Their brains had rewired to alter the way they dealt with the light entering their eyeballs. Despite the glasses inverting everything they saw, their brains flipped the image 180 degrees so they could function normally again!

Dumbfounded, NASA repeated the tests on fresh subjects, only this time half of them removed their glasses on day 14 for a few hours. In the group that kept them on for a month, the subjects' brains altered the image within 25 to 30 days. In the group who removed their glasses for a few hours on day 14, it took a further 25 to 30 days before their brains reversed the image entering their eyes.

The experiment has been repeated often, and every time it proves conclusively that our brains take 25 to 30 days to form a new habit—about the time it takes for the moon to cycle in its orbit.

This is a *crucial* point to remember once you've finished reading this book and begin actively creating your own fantastic world. When we set a goal, and take daily action in visualizing that goal intensely, as if it were already real, we do so for at least a month.

Our physical brains set about creating new neural pathways, new behaviours and habits that will help to bring about these things we think about.

You will begin to consciously plan every aspect of your life, think about it repeatedly, experience it in your mind, and then watch it become real in front of your very eyes. It's awesome.

PRIORITY SEVEN

Another tip I would like to pass on, one that works wonderfully on keeping you focussed on daily action, is what I call my Priority Seven.

Every night, before I go to bed, I make a list of all the things I need to do the next day. I used to do this with a pen and paper, but now use the Notepad function on my computer or a list-making application on my phone.

This is typically a list of ten or more items that need doing, and perhaps some longer term goals. It might look like this:

Post the application form

Mow the lawn

Cut neighbour's hedge

Order that new book on Amazon

Apply undercoat to new door frames

Apply first coat of gloss to door frames
Answer email from J Smith
Spend an hour writing the new book
Write to P Brown to invite to lunch
Go to the gym
Go shopping for fresh five-bean chilli ingredients
Cook dinner (five-bean chilli)
Take Billy swimming
Pay electricity bill online (overdue)
Find online coaching course
Purchase online coaching course
Call Mum, remind her I love her

Next, I rearrange them in order of priority, numbering only the first seven items:

1. Spend an hour writing the new book
2. Apply undercoat to new door frames
3. Pay electricity bill online (overdue)
4. Answer email from J Smith
5. Write to P Brown to invite to lunch
6. Call Mum, remind her I love her
7. Apply first coat of gloss to door frames
   Take Billy swimming
   Cut neighbour's hedge
   Post the application form
   Go to the gym
   Go shopping for fresh five-bean chilli ingredients
   Cook dinner (five-bean chilli)
   Mow the lawn
   Order that new book on Amazon
   Find online coaching course
   Purchase online coaching course

Perhaps on my final look, I realize that after undercoating all of the door frames, the next four tasks (paying a bill online, answering a few emails, posting a letter, calling Mum) would not give enough time for the undercoat to dry, in order for me to complete task seven, painting the frames with gloss. So I simply go to the next task, 'take Billy swimming', and paint the frames after.

At the end of that busy day, when I come to write my Priority Seven for the following day, today's list would look like this:

1. Spend an hour writing the new book
2. Apply undercoat to new door frames
3. Pay electricity bill online (overdue)
4. Answer email from J Smith
5. Write to P Brown to invite to lunch
6. Call Mum, remind her I love her
7. Take Billy swimming
    Apply first coat of gloss to door frames
    Cut neighbour's hedge
    Post the application form
    Go to the gym
    Go shopping for fresh five-bean chilli ingredients
    Cook dinner (five-bean chilli)
    Mow the lawn
    Order that new book on Amazon
    Find online coaching course
    Purchase online coaching course

I would then rename the file, changing it from 'Priority Seven – 15 March' to 'Priority Seven – 16 March'. I can now delete today's tasks, forget them, and quickly move things around. Within seconds, my list looks like this:

1. Spend an hour writing the new book
2. Apply first coat of gloss to door frames

3. Cut neighbour's hedge
4. Post the application form
5. Go to the gym
6. Go shopping for fresh five-bean chilli ingredients
7. Cook dinner (five-bean chilli)
    Mow the lawn
    Order that new book on Amazon
    Find online coaching course
    Purchase online coaching course

The key with this method, once you have your list sorted, is to look only at number 1, and not give a moment's thought to number 2 on your list.

Only when number 1 is completed for the day do you move to the next thing on your list, number 2, and then you don't give a moment's thought to the next task, until you've completed number 2, and so forth.

Notice how I added 'Spend an hour writing the new book' as the most important task on both days. That's because that might be the most important task to keep doing until the book is completed. So, it will always be task 1 until completed, a daily task.

Notice also that I placed a 'charitable task' in my Priority Seven: 'Call Mum, remind her I love her' or 'Cut neighbour's hedge'. Wherever possible, try to do at least one thing every single day that adds to the life of another person, however small you might perceive any effect to be—dropping some small change into a charity collection box at the supermarket checkout, donating some clothes to a charity shop, helping an elderly neighbour, calling a family member who you haven't seen or spoken to for a while.

Not only will you feel great about doing something so positive, but you will rewire your brain to do so, until it becomes a habit. Remember those astronauts and their strange glasses? Make it a habit to help someone in any way, every single day, and it will become second nature to you.

Then watch your life improve as a direct result. 'What goes around, comes around.' You'll see!

People often ask me how on earth I cram so much into my life. Now you know.

I retired that night like a king to his bedchamber. Full and fulfilled, with a feeling of unthinkable wealth. Not of the monetary kind, of course, but of new-found knowledge and the confidence that it brings.

My first parachute instructor reminded me to listen carefully on my training day, because knowledge dispels fear. Indeed, that was the parachute training school's motto.

'Knowledge dispels fear'. How true.

My new-found knowledge tucked me into bed that night with a heady mix of nervousness and excitement for what might follow.

Tomorrow was summit day. The weather, I'd been assured, was favourable, and the only thing that lay between my bed and the summit was my strength of mind.

That night, it was as strong as an ox.

I could taste victory. All I had to do was rise early and make it happen.

CHAPTER SEVEN

*"Flow with whatever is happening
and let your mind be free."*

— ZHUANGZI *(369–286 BC), CHINESE PHILOSOPHER*

Allow

By the time Pierce tapped his wooden walking stick on my door at 5 a.m., I was already packed, warmed up and ready to go.

An air of seriousness followed us from the purple temple as we left in near darkness to hit the trail early. Although our chatter was polite and uplifting, the delayed pauses between comments exposed an excited nervousness about the day ahead.

This was summit day. The culmination of a hard week of trekking, this day should be victory day, and yet many potential challenges lay ahead.

Pierce had said little about the route to the final pinnacle of the mountain. All I knew was that we were not going to be using ropes and steel ladders, and that ice shoes were not required. Still, I knew it was going to be a tough walk, in which I'd have to dig deep.

To my amazement, I was walking now in perfect shape. Only the shortness of breath remained, as my lungs were not yet fully accustomed to breathing at those lofty heights.

After descending into a small valley, the trail quickly headed upwards once more, a very gradual spiral that was steep and constant. We ascended ever upward until we were squinting at the morning sun reflected from a blanket of virgin snow. Within two hours, our pace had slowed to a crawl.

With each step, my feet felt like they were getting heavier, harder to lift. In the same way that a person's boots collect more wet mud as they walk over a soggy field, so my boots seemed to be getting heavier and heavier as time slowly passed.

I dug deep and caught Pierce up, the path now being wide enough for us to walk side by side. "The weather's looking fine this morning," I said, "clear blue sky, no wind."

"It is. Perfect."

"So you think we have a good chance of reaching the summit today?"

"I know we will. That is, I fully *expect* us to. I have no doubt in my mind at all. Therefore, we shall summit today."

"I admire your confidence," I laughed. "I'll go along with that then, and look forward to getting there."

"All you have to do, my friend, is *allow*."

"Of course," I said, not really understanding what he meant, but not wanting to sound stupid.

Pierce looked at me for several paces. "We have discussed much on this mountain," he began, "and perhaps this is the final instruction for the recipe I am trying to pass on to you."

Pierce gave me a warm smile.

"The secrets I have shared with you on this mountain could be likened to the ingredients of a cake. You have added them to the bowl, you have mixed them together, and you have placed them in a warm oven. What, my dear friend, happens next?"

"The cake bakes in the oven?"

"It does indeed, but what action must you take now, having mixed the ingredients and placed them in the oven?"

"Come back when it's done? I'm not sure I understand what you're getting at."

"Well, the answer is simple. You must wait."

"I knew that," I said smiling, wiping a bead of sweat from my brow. "Do go on."

"You must *allow* the cake to rise and cook. If you fully trust the recipe, and fully trust the oven is working correctly, do you pace in front of the oven, worrying if it is burning? Or do you concern yourself with whether it will taste terrible or not?"

"No, not if I'm familiar with the oven and followed the recipe correctly."

"Exactly!" Pierce replied, flicking his stick in the air, sending a marble of snow down the mountain. "And if it needed an hour in the oven, would you open the door after five minutes to see how it was doing, and let all the heat escape?"

"I wouldn't."

"Precisely!" Pierce replied. "Precisely. Do you then try to turn the heat of the oven up to speed up the cooking of the cake?"

"No, that would burn the outside of the cake and leave the middle uncooked."

"*Exactly!*" Pierce shouted, as he stopped still for the first time in several hours. "Why then, do we not sit back and let our dreams become reality, as the chef sits back to let his cake cook?"

I had no reply, and could only shrug my shoulders as I inhaled deeply, taking full advantage of the stop.

"We talked about one of the greatest Universal Laws, the Law of Attraction, and how sustained thoughts and feelings attract situations to us that match those thoughts and feelings. We discussed our godlike ability to create our own future.

"I told you to set worthy goals, and to visualize those goals while relaxing. I explained that the best form of relaxation is meditation, and suggested you plant those thought seeds into the fertile soil of your subconscious mind, by repeated and consistent daily practice, for at least one month, without missing a single day.

"We spoke of gratitude, and what an important part of the creation process this is. How happy and grateful we must be, for *all* the good in our lives, for the greatness around us now, and for the amazing things on their way to us.

"I asked you to observe what followed, to notice the coincidences, to notice noticing the many coincidences that follow when you live your life 'by design'.

"I urged you to take action, massive action, on the many elements that flow into your life following the selection of a worthy goal, meditation, visualization, gratitude and observation.

"My final instruction is to simply *allow*. Sending your heartfelt desire out into the Universe is like placing the cake mixture into the hot oven. Treat it in the same way. Know that your dreams are coming, just as surely as you would know the cake would cook perfectly and taste great.

"There are Universal Laws at play, and you cannot bend them. The Law of Gestation is the law that allows a human baby to form in nine months, and a giant oak tree in 100 years. We cannot form a perfect baby in nine days, any more than we can grow a mighty oak tree in ten years. There is a gestation period for every seed correctly planted in the eternally powerful resources of the subconscious mind.

"There is also a Law of Rhythm, a time for all things, 'a time to reap and a time to sow'. That is why turning up the temperature of the oven will not bake the perfect cake any faster."

"I'm confused," I confessed. "You seem to be telling me to be patient, and yet you're telling me to send my request out into the Universe every day, for at least a month, but ideally until it becomes real."

Pierce smiled, paused, and nodded, as he began to slowly walk once more up the steep snowy bank.

"I understand your confusion, my friend. It appears at first to be a paradox, and yet it really is nothing of the sort. Imagine, if you will, that you decide to update your car, and you choose a shiny red sports car.

"Following my advice, you seek images of the exact car you desire, from magazines and sales brochures. If you follow my advice carefully, you will go so far as to visit a car showroom, and test drive the car, perhaps have your photograph taken behind the wheel. Better still, perhaps you take a photograph from behind the wheel, to help you visualize yourself driving your next car.

"After this period, you choose a date to begin the manifestation of your new desire. Let us say that you choose to begin a couple of days before the full moon, knowing you will visualize this goal until the next full moon.

"Now, in answer to your question, you are correct: you do not sit down in a quiet place, and visualize owning the car, as if you already own it, and do nothing else.

"You send out that vibe of gratitude that you own the red sports car, and you imagine yourself driving it, filling it with fuel, taking trips out, chatting to your passenger, visiting the shops, washing the car on a sunny day, lovingly polishing and shining the paint work. You bring in all of your senses, the smell of the leather seats, and the sound of the engine purring, the dazzling imagery and the feel of the steering wheel in your hands.

"After a couple of days, when the images start to become familiar, they start to feel like memories. They start to feel real. The daily visualizations you will perform during your meditations or quiet periods are to reinforce that feeling.

"Never doubt that you will own that red sports car, because a moment of doubt, left unchecked, stops the cogs of the great Universal Machine in its tracks. If you keep thinking those doubtful thoughts, you set the great machine into reverse and your dream car begins to fade. Reject the opinions of all those that would lead you astray, and accuse you of dreaming.

"Rather, become a beacon to light the way for those around you, for you can demonstrate the reality of these great laws in no better way than by example."

"Thanks, Pierce. I get it. I'm to visualize often, and live my life as if I know it's coming, giving time to let Nature do its thing. While I remain focussed and excited about the fact it's going to happen."

"Follow the advice I have given you previously," Pierce continued, "in noticing the coincidences that begin to occur. Explore every new opportunity that drifts your way. There is every chance that these 'random occurrences' are stepping stones to the realization of your dream. Take action!

"Let the Universe work through you to bring that great idea from the spiritual realm of thoughts and ideas, to the physical realm you are enjoying right now."

"I can't wait to get started with creating my new life on purpose," I said to Pierce, struggling to breathe in the ice-cold air.

"Indeed. Have you tried to picture what it will look like when we reach the very top today? More importantly, have you imagined how that is going to feel?"

"Of course!"

"Then your journey has already begun, my dear, dear friend, it has already begun," he smiled. "Now, stop and close your eyes—I have a surprise for you."

I resisted the temptation to peek like a five-year-old, and assumed it was a test of trust. I would have counted on Pierce in any situation, so I closed my eyes and waited expectantly.

He spun me around clumsily, muttering and laughing to himself under his breath as he did so.

"There, open your eyes. Our resting place," he declared, like a proud wizard showing off to a startled apprentice.

It took a little while for me to focus and get used to the bright sunlight reflecting from the snowy scene before me. When it came into focus, I was so shocked that I almost gasped aloud.

I became overwhelmed with emotion. I tried to rationalize that it was an effect of the altitude—I'd felt tearful on previous climbs where the ascent was rapid. However, in all honesty I knew this was different; this was something powerful and deeply spiritual.

Resting in Heaven

Ahead of us rose a palatial temple of pure brilliant white, sparkling like ice. A construction of such grandeur looked out of place in one of the most remote locations I had ever visited.

Drawing closer, I observed that the structure was built entirely from solid stone, from smooth white marble that glistened in the late morning sun. I couldn't begin to imagine how these large stones could have been transported up this challenging mountain, and yet there they were. It must have taken centuries to complete.

Thoughts of reaching the summit quickly evaporated, replaced instead by a longing to see the inside of this magnificent structure. I'd been welcomed at every temple on our route, and knew that superb hospitality awaited, perhaps some food and drink, and maybe even somewhere to take a nap until we were ready to push for the summit.

The large wooden doors were inlaid with much gold leaf and ornate carving, the building entrance looming over us like a freshly constructed Parthenon.

I turned to ask Pierce where we should knock on the door. He grinned at my excitement. He held out his arm; no sooner had I stepped forward than the doors shook loudly, trembling as they began to open inwards.

"We have been watching you, curious visitor, and we are eager to help you rest a while," said a small, gentle man wearing white robes and a cream coloured cloak that dragged behind him on the floor.

"Thank you," I replied. "You are most kind."

"This way, my friend, this way."

I was becoming used to the temple workers ignoring poor Pierce and treating me so well. I was sure they had fun with Pierce for he seemed to spend all of his time in their company, in all of the temples we had visited. I followed my host through the roofed entrance, on through some tall white marble columns and into the first courtyard, my eyes widening at the glorious splendour.

Every stone was so precisely cut that you would struggle to push a playing card between the joins. Every corner was precisely 90 degrees and every surface as smooth as ice, as if the whole place had been sanded down from blocks of white chalk.

The people I passed moved with an air of grace and dignity. All of them wore the cleanest white robes, their heartfelt joy radiating from them like sunbeams through a misty wood.

"Please rest here, and rejuvenate. Can I bring you tea?" said the temple worker, as he bowed low and stepped backwards, motioning towards a large white door before me.

"That's most kind," I replied. "Thank you."

"Please make yourself at home," he smiled, before gliding off in the direction we had just walked.

The room behind the white door was as surprisingly grand as the white temple itself. It had no en suite bathroom and widescreen TV on the wall, and yet felt more lavish than any five star hotel I'd ever stayed in. The room was spacious, clean, and somehow warm. The large bed was raised from the floor, and supported a thick mattress.

The windows had shutters, both inside and outside to keep out the weather and the noise, or to be opened to let in the sunshine or a cool breeze.

Ancient parchments in wooden frames decorated the whitewashed walls, depicting ancient study of the sun's movement across the skies, the phases of the moon, and the movement of stars through various seasons. Some parchments demonstrated an advanced medical knowledge, while others showed maps of far-flung places unknown to me on modern maps.

By the time I'd thrown down my rucksack, removed my boots and changed my socks, my green tea had arrived. I thanked the young man who delivered it, and as he opened the door to leave, Pierce approached.

"How cool is this place?" I said. "And the people, they all seem so happy and relaxed."

"That will be because they are," he laughed. "They enjoy the wonderful feeling of freedom that knowledge allows. They are filled with great love and powerful gratitude for their amazing lives. Full of appreciation for what most people take for granted. They live a glorious life of passion, enthusiastic about what they are doing and excited about what the Universe will deliver to them next."

I nodded in wonder, nursing my hot tea, which seemed to warm not only my body but my mind and soul.

"When you have finished your quenching tea, my friend, you should slip on your boots. I have something I would very much like to show you."

The Centre of the Crown

Pierce led me across the courtyard as he explained the plan for the remainder of the day.

We were to make the final ascent two hours before sunset when the winds were likely to settle and the cloud cover dissipate. Pierce walked fast, keen to show me around, this being the last temple we'd experience together on the trip. He had, he explained, something 'rather special' to show me.

I peeped into the occasional doorway as we passed various temple buildings that twinkled like ice sculptures in the afternoon sun. Each was serene, the people whispering to each other with love and laughter, or meditating with blissful smiles on their faces. All was very peaceful.

We slipped between two white buildings and emerged onto an impressive courtyard, the centrepiece to the whole temple.

I blinked hard to make sure I wasn't seeing things. What I saw seemed even more out of place for the top of a mountain than the temple itself. At the heart of this white temple stood a unique and remarkable structure. It looked, at first glance, like an old round observatory with a domed roof. Only instead of standing on the ground, it stood seven feet off the floor on seven stone pillars.

Access to the building, which had a diameter of about 22 feet, was via a ladder, which was slightly wider at the bottom than it was at the top.

The domed roof was smooth, and there were magical symbols deeply carved into each of the seven supporting pillars. Walking closer, I noticed a very peculiar thing. At the base of each column was a small pond of cold water: the pillars actually stood in water!

"What are the pillars made of?" I asked Pierce, who stood beside me with his hands on his hips, his bearded chin raised with a sense of pride at the monument he was sharing with me. "It doesn't quite look like the same white marble the rest of the temple is built from, is it?"

"No," Pierce replied. "It is a softer, more brittle material, chosen for its ease of carving, and also because of its delicate nature. Believe it or not, they actually want to have to maintain these pillars each day."

"Why? Why on earth would you build such a..."

"Because the structure before you, as well as being a practical space for deep meditation, is also reminding the temple inhabitants of one of the key secrets of life.

"The architect was inspired in a dream to suspend the monument on seven pillars in such a way that if even just one of them were to collapse, the entire structure would come crashing down."

"Wow! Has that ever happened?"

"No. Never. They take great care each and every day to look after this building, for it represents their own lives."

I looked quizzically towards Pierce, before returning my gaze back to the fantastic structure.

"You see, your life on this earth might be likened to such a fantastic monument. It is supported by seven pillars and, as you can see, each of those columns rests in a pool of water. Now imagine that one of the pools started to freeze. It is certainly cold enough up here for them to do so. Because the pillars are quite brittle, the freezing pool would cause the column to crack, and the weight of the structure above would cause that pillar to implode. Disaster!

"A plan was implemented here in the White Temple to make sure that never happens. Each morning as the sun rises, the High Priest carries a ceremonial vessel of boiling water to the base of each pillar and pours it into the pool of water. He then returns with a basket of pure salt crystals, which he sprinkles into each of the warm water pools. The High Priest repeats this action twice more: once at midday, and again at sunset.

"The sacred building now rests on seven pillars, which rest in seven pools of warm, salty water."

The Seven Pillars of Life

"We really can liken our lives to this great building. Your life has supporting pillars that need to be lovingly maintained. If any of these columns are neglected and allowed to freeze and crack, then the building, your life, begins to freeze and crack, and left unchecked, would begin to collapse around you."

"I see," I replied, trying to take it all in. "And I'm guessing each of those magical symbols relates to different aspects of our lives, right? I notice they're all different."

"Yes," Pierce replied. "The one to the right of the ladder is the Physical Pillar, representing the majestic monument to creation that is your physical body. We serve this well by the eating of good, clean food, and by the regular exercising of our muscles and organs."

Pierce walked around to the second pillar, to the right of the first.

"This," he continued, "is the Mind Pillar. The rain-drop that eventually becomes the raging river, the small spark that becomes the forest fire, our minds are the creative epicentre of our own world. We nourish this pillar by learning, by reading the great books written by the wise and inspired. We plant the image seeds of a life that is yet to be, and water them with continuous heartfelt love and gratitude. We thus stretch and exercise our minds like our bodies, and open it to untold possibilities."

Pierce walked anti-clockwise around the structure. "The third column is the Financial Pillar—as important in its own way as any other pillar, but not more important. Most of the prayers that drift out into the ether, regardless of faith, cry out for more money. 'If only I had more money, I could put more food on the table.' 'If I had more money I could finally have that holiday I have been promising the family for so long.'

"There is nothing at all wrong with wanting to be wealthy. Having money opens doors and allows you to live the life you were born to live. Indeed, I strongly recommend that you pursue money.

"Having said that, I should also point out that this third pillar is no larger than any of the others. It is equally as important as your physical health and mental health, for example, but not more important. Nor is it more important than your relationships with those you love. It is one aspect of the whole, an important supporting column that keeps the building of life standing strong and tall, in all its glory.

"The fourth column is the Pillar of Spiritual Growth. Please do not confuse or limit this to any religious beliefs you might have. Spiritual growth relates to your extremely personal connection to the Universe, however you perceive that to be. It might be witnessed in a piece of beautiful music that touches your soul and brings a tear to your eye. It might be the unexpected rush of raw emotion that occurs when watching two people who love each other take their wedding vows. Parents often feel it with the first cry of a newborn child, others by an unexpected charitable act or show of love.

"Spiritual Growth is about opening your spiritual eyes to a world of wonder and amazement and your spiritual ears to the whispers of inspiration.

"Whether you realize it yet or not, this journey we have made together has assisted you greatly in widening those spiritual eyes, and helped you to listen more carefully to that still, small voice. It has brought you one step closer to connecting with the intelligent, loving conscious Universe."

I nodded at Pierce and smiled the way a student might grin to a great teacher on graduation day. I was already seeing the world in a new light and already tuning in to that still, small voice within.

I pointed at the magical symbols on the fifth pillar. "What about this one, Pierce? We've had Physical, Mind, Financial, Spiritual. What's this one?"

"This represents relationships. Literally translated the fifth column is the Interaction Pillar. It is about the way you interact with yourself and with others. Do you give yourself the time you deserve? Are you sometimes a little harsh with yourself? How do you interact with your family, your partner, your children, and your parents?

"This pillar reminds you to devote time and energy into glowing like a candle so that others will be attracted to you, like moths to your flickering flame.

"The sixth support over here is the Charitable Pillar. Did you know that the more we give, the more we receive? This particular pillar is so often abandoned in the modern world! Selfishness and cold-heartedness cause the pool to freeze quickly, as the cracks appear and the heavy building above threatens to topple down like a house of cards.

"As we give of our time, our expertise, and our finances, with a sincere gesture of giving and simply for the joy of giving, an amazing thing happens. It comes back to us. Often it comes back to us manifold. Seemingly from nowhere, people give you their time and attention. Money arrives in the post or into your bank, or opportunities arise seemingly out of nowhere.

"Charity and service to others are such an important pillar, a pillar supporting your glorious life. Please do not neglect it! Lovingly give, and stand by to graciously receive."

Pierce and I continued our slow walk around the building, until we stopped where we had first arrived, right in front of the circular structure. This time Pierce pointed his walking stick to the left of the ladder, to the seventh supporting pillar.

"Finally, this last column. It is the Gratitude Pillar. As we have already discussed, all too often overlooked in this life is the immense power of saying 'thank you'. Sincerely thank the people in your life every day for all the little things they do. Not just your family—the postman, the taxi driver, the waitress, the cashier—all of the people, be grateful to them, and be grateful *for* them.

"Look to the stars and be grateful for all aspects of your life. Send out that loving vibration of thanks for your physical and mental well-being, for the money you do have and the money on its way, for the spiritual side of life that opens up to you more and more each day.

"Give thanks for those relationships in your past, for they helped you to become the exceptional human being you are today. Give thanks for the relationships you have in your life today; breathe them in and enjoy every aspect of the interaction. Give gratitude for the relationships that are yet to be, for as you shine like a bright new penny, so will you attract to you all the good people who will complete your wonderful life.

"Finally, give thanks for the opportunities that come your way to help others. Be grateful for those that can benefit from your wise words and actions, who appreciate that little time and attention that makes them grow. Give thanks for the avenues that widen before you, that you may donate and contribute to improving the lives of your fellow travellers on this amazing, living Earth."

We stood for a moment, gazing at the pillars before us, until Pierce broke the silence. "So there, my dear friend, we have it. Seven key aspects of your life, each with *equal* importance, each distributing the load, each as crucial as the next. Neglect any one of these aspects, and the whole structure weakens. Abandon any one of these pillars, and eventually the building, your life, will collapse around you.

"We must give equal attention to the development of our minds, our bodies, our finances, our spirituality, our interaction with others, our charitable endeavours, and our sincere gratitude."

With that Pierce clapped his hands loudly, as if awakening me from a trance.

"Come!" he shouted. "We must eat. I have arranged for food to be taken to your room."

We quickly retraced our steps between the two buildings and past numerous other structures.

"We have a date with the summit of this beautiful mountain," Pierce said with a smile, "and I do not want to let her down. The sun grows low in the sky. We leave in one hour."

The Final Push

Despite being tired and having just eaten a delicious meal, washed down with mountain spring water, I found it impossible to take a quick nap that afternoon.

My mind went over the whole 'seven pillars' idea that Pierce had shared with me. When I wasn't thinking about that, I was mixing fear with excitement as I imagined myself summiting within the next couple of hours.

Remarkably, by the time Pierce and I had left the white temple and started our final push, I didn't have a tired bone in my body. Only seven days ago I was suffering with a terrible cold, headaches, coughing, and a runny nose. My back was hurting, and my aching legs and blisters were driving me to distraction. Seven days on, as I neared the summit, only a slight breathlessness remained.

Usually a person's health was more likely to deteriorate as they ascended a mountain. In my case, the higher I got, the better I seemed to feel. Brilliant.

As we stopped the steep climb for a moment to skirt around a large icy overhang, I regained my breath enough to talk in a quiet voice.

"Thanks, Pierce," I said. "Thanks for showing me those amazing temples this week. That last one, the white temple, really was something else."

"I agree," Pierce said with a twinkle in his eye. "It really is the crown of this beautiful mountain."

"Why do you refer to the white temple as the crown of the mountain, Pierce? Isn't the summit its crown?"

Pierce grinned and nodded, before stopping in his tracks. He almost spoke to me, but then hesitated.

"This way," he said. "This next stage is tough on the old legs, so let us take it nice and easy. Slowly, slowly."

He dug his stick into the thick snow, and began heading up the 45 degree slope. A brief silence followed, as Pierce seemed to mull things over in his mind. Then he spoke.

"My friend. Are you familiar with energy?"

"I'm not sure what you mean," I replied, "but I certainly hope I have enough in reserve to reach the top. This is tough going."

Pierce screwed up his face, digging in hard with his stick and the toes of his boots through the icy coating on the snow.

"What I meant was, do you understand that everything around us is energy?"

"Go on," I said, happy to listen and focus on my breathing.

"Well, the mountain itself is made of energy, the snow underneath our feet, the boots we wear, our entire bodies, are all made from the same substance. Energy. The only real difference between one thing and another is the speed and magnitude at which it vibrates."

"Really?"

"Yes. I will explain a little more in a moment if you wish. I want to answer your question about the 'crown' of the mountain first."

"Please," I said, reduced to one-word answers by the rarefied air.

"Your body has seven energy centres that run through it, like mini whirlwinds of energy, called 'chakras'. They are invisible to the naked eye of most people, operating a little outside of our perceptual range. If you could see my chakras right now, they would look like swirling circles of light, at least from the front and back.

"That is to say, if you lay on your back and I observed these energy centres from your side, they would look like mini tornados, seven of them in total. One between your legs, five spinning on the body, one spinning on your head.

"They whirl from the front getting smaller and smaller, until they touch a point inside your body, then spin larger and larger out through the back of you."

I stopped to catch my breath.

"I have confused you?"

"Yes," I said, followed by a sharp intake of breath through the nose, and a slow continuous outward breath from my mouth. "Maybe it's the altitude."

"Imagine I grabbed a large funnel some six feet wide, which tapered to a sharp point. And imagine I stuck that right through the centre of your chest."

"Ouch."

"Yes, I know, but bear with me. Now imagine I got an identical funnel, and stuck it in your back, right between your shoulder blades. That would be the shape and position of your heart chakra. The word 'chakra' comes from the Sanskrit for 'wheel' or 'spinning'.

"The heart chakra, if you could see it with your physical eyes, is green. It is actually green with flashes of pink swirling through it, but for the sake of simplicity, consider it green.

"As I explained, my friend, we have seven main chakras: a red one at the bottom of the scale, spinning out of your groin towards the earth, an orange chakra around your belly button, and a yellow chakra around your solar plexus, the area directly below your breastbone.

Higher than that, we have the green heart chakra I just mentioned, located right in the middle of your chest.

Higher still is the blue energy spiral at the throat, then the lilac or purple brow chakra located directly between your eyebrows. Finally, spiralling from the very top of your head, we have the crown chakra, an energy point of brilliant white connecting you to the Source of all energy."

"And you believe all this stuff, Pierce?" I quizzed, as we slowly began to walk again. "You believe it literally?"

"My friend, I know it to be true. I have spent so much time with the elders of these parts, and I speak the truth. I am able to speed up my chakras as easily as spinning a wheel on an overturned cart. That is why I referred to the white temple as the crown of the mountain."

"Oh, I see," I replied. "Because it's white and…"

That's when it hit me. That's when it dawned on me how the temples were all somehow linked.

"How stupid am I?" I barked at Pierce, struggling to maintain my footing up the slippery mountain.

"Stupid?"

"You just told me the first chakra, the earthy one…"

"The root chakra."

"Yes, you just told me the root chakra was red, right? And the first temple was red. I never realized that! Like the rainbow, we went from red temple to orange temple, orange to yellow, yellow to green, green to blue, blue to purple, and purple temple to white temple."

Pierce chuckled as I stated the obvious. "We did indeed."

"And so you're saying, these people, the ones who built these villages and temples, they knew this, right?" I paused to catch my breath again, and placed my gloved hands on my hips as I bent over to breathe.

"Of course. The builders knew. As I told you yesterday, legend says a tall bearded white man gave them the plans and ideas, and they knew the links and symbolism in and between the various temples. Today, not everyone who lives on the mountain knows the order of things, for they were built long ago.

"Many people from the lower temples are not even aware of the higher temples, others know of their existence through stories, but have never visited them. Many have little desire to do so, too concerned with the reality they see as their everyday lives.

"Yes, as we climb the mountain through the various temples, we can liken that to the rise through the various energy centres of the body. And the comparisons do not end there, my friend."

Vibrational Attitude

"The red root chakra, connected as it is to the earth, is a lower energy. It vibrates at a lower rate. The crown chakra, connected as it is to Source, spins at a faster rate and a greater rate of vibration," Pierce explained.

"So we're back to vibration. You were going to explain that," I interrupted like an impatient schoolchild.

"Indeed I was, my friend. I shall explain in a moment. Before I do, I wanted to draw your attention to something else you may have missed as you climbed this mountain. I would like you to understand it before we reach the top, for we are near."

Every cell in my tired body leapt for joy at the notion of being close to the top. I could see the sun was approaching the horizon, but hadn't dared to hope we could be close to the very summit of this majestic mountain.

"The red root chakra," he continued, "is vibrating at a lower rate, while the crown chakra vibrates at a much higher rate. The chakras in between gradually speed up as they move from red to orange, orange to yellow, and so on, until we reach the crown.

"Not only the temple colours tie in with the body's energy centres, but the inhabitants of the villages and temples."

"How do you mean?"

"Well, consider the people you observed at the village of the red temple. Do you remember them?"

"Yes, I do. It feels like a month ago, but yes, I do remember because it was the first temple I'd seen, and I wasn't expecting to be staying in

. The people were a bit negative, I didn't really feel welcome."

remember well. The people there can be nasty to each other, and despair and mistrust fill their souls. They are plagued with guilt and fear, forgetting their ability to change their destinies. You must recall then, when you think back, the ever so slight change in the people we met outside the next temple, the orange temple?"

"To be honest, Pierce," I replied, "not really. They seemed very similar, a little hostile and suspicious."

"Let me ask another question," Pierce suggested, as we slowly began our ascent once more. "We mentioned hostility, despair and mistrust at the red temple. Did you witness any of those things at the white temple?"

"No, of course not."

"When you compare the red temple to the white temple, the difference is vast, like night and day. As we climbed the mountain, we witnessed the raising of a vibration, only it was so subtle that you did not notice it until now.

"Had we wanted to ascend straight from the shoddiness of the red temple to the grandeur of the white temple in a single bound, we would have failed. The *only* way to reach the white temple is to travel the route we just walked together this past week.

"We *had to* move from the red temple up to the orange temple, orange temple to yellow and so on, all the way from the purple temple up to the wonderful white temple.

"As in life, there is no real short cut. The path you walked is the only way, and you had a whirlwind tour. Most people would take twice as long to trek the path you just took. Fortunately, you had me with you and, knowing the mountain like the back of my wrinkled hand, I got you up here in seven days. And we are nearly at the top, I can feel it."

"I can't wait," I said, gasping for air in this cold place at the top of the world. Then I planted my right foot onto a patch of hard frozen snow and it slipped. I banged my knee hard and winced in pain.

"Careful, careful," said Pierce. "We have come too far to have to turn back now. Besides, we do not want you triggering an avalanche, do we? I do not think our friends below in the white temple would approve, do you?"

He smiled, baring his yellowed teeth beneath his grey-white beard, and then continued, as if remembering an important point.

"You know, the avalanche reminds us of how quickly we can fall back down to lower places. Like our little tumble the other day, we were lucky not to be swept right back down the mountain to where we started.

"Life, like this wonderful mountain, is just the same. If we allow ourselves to get caught up in things that distract us, if we cease to take action, or begin to mix with people who would rock our beliefs or weaken our faith, we slide downhill rapidly."

"I get that," I said. "It reminds me a little of that dream I had the other day."

"I was about to say the selfsame thing," Pierce grinned. "First, however, allow me to explain what I meant when I referred to frequency and vibration. The summit draws near."

Pierce took a sharp intake of breath, and adopted a serious look. "Do you remember the pools of water that housed the pillars that supported that domed building back there? Imagine if the High Priest failed to add the boiling water and salt three times a day."

"They would freeze."

"Yes. Which means the molecules in the water have slowed down a little. Imagine, if you will, a cauldron of water, rather than a pool of water. We know that with a very powerful microscope we could see that the water is actually made up of billions of tiny molecules. If we were to take our cauldron of water up here on the mountain with us, the vibrating molecules making up the water would slow down, so much so that the water would turn into ice.

"What was once a fluid thing, would now be a fixed, seemingly static thing. Of course, it is still vibrating, but the molecules are vibrating more slowly. And the atoms that make up the molecules are vibrating, as are all the tiny parts inside the atom, and the tiny components inside the tiny parts!

"When the ice melts at room temperature, the molecules are vibrating faster again. If we place our cauldron on a fire, the water molecules vibrate faster and faster until the water turns into steam.

"It is all water, right? Yet we created three seemingly different substances: ice, water and steam. All we did is change the rate of vibration.

"All of these oscillating items create this illusion we call the physical world, in this case, water. Everything is vibrating—the water, the cauldron containing the water, your hand holding the cauldron by its handle."

The Current

"Another Universal Law, the Law of Polarity, can be likened to this. The ice would be over on the negative side, at a lower vibration, the water in the neutral midway point, and the steam at the higher vibration on the positive side.

"Feelings follow the Law of Polarity. For example, when we learn of an earthquake, some people will wonder how many people perished, even see this as a sign of 'the end of days'. Others will feel neutral: these things happen all of the time, and the inhabitants knew they were living in an earthquake zone. Others will have a positive outlook: thank goodness the people knew in advance and evacuated the city; they marvel at the modern earthquake-proof homes, and look in wonder at the power and majesty of planet Earth.

"It is like your dream. You made the worst island full of thunder and lightning, with a massive erupting volcano. To some, this would be heaven; how many people get to watch a real volcano erupting and feel the ground move beneath their feet?

"Likewise, the island you called 'heavenly' might appear lazy and unproductive to others; lazing around in the sunshine eating grapes is not everyone's idea of fun. Some people despise lounging around in the sun all day!

"One final point: I believe an inspired aspect of your dream was the strong current drifting right to left, or from east to west. It meant the only way you could get back to the good islands was to follow the 'V' shape back down to where you started, then head to the right again from good island to better island."

"Why inspired?" I asked, closing my eyes for a moment, and slowly bringing my breathing under control.

"Because in life, we cannot jump from despair to joy in a single bound. In the same way that we could not jump from the hostility felt around the red temple to the love experienced at the white temple. As I have explained, it is all about baby steps.

"Generally speaking, a human being cannot be suicidal one moment, and then overjoyed a moment later. A suicidal man might raise his frequency, his vibration from suicidal to deeply depressed. The deeply depressed person cannot wake up in bliss, but he can move to a place of depression. And so it goes, one step at a time, gradually raising one's frequency, focussing on the end goal and taking daily action in that direction.

"By the time the man 'feeling a bit down' has increased his vibration to 'feeling okay', he gets out of his home and feels the sun on his face, starts to meet people, starts to talk, and slowly his vibration rises and he moves in the direction of peace and abundance.

"And so it was in your dream. From the beginning, we had to move from the bottom of the 'V' formation of islands, to the first island on the right. We could not sail straight to Heavenly Isle, but instead had to make the journey in stages, one island at a time.

"To get from where we are now, to where we want to be, we must act in a certain way, moving forward in little steps. Knowing all of the time that things are getting better and better. However, we become lazy at our own peril, for if we cease to take inspired action towards the goals of our dreams, so we risk shipwreck, and having to start all over again."

On Top of the World

I smiled at Pierce. I was happy for various reasons.

Firstly, I finally understood what he was trying to convey to me.

Secondly, I felt good that I'd had a dream on the mountain, one I could recall the next day, and one that actually meant something.

Thirdly, I could sense the climax of the journey was very close indeed.

The sky had slowly grown bigger over the last hour, whilst the mountain up and in front of me had become smaller and smaller.

"We are moments away, my friend," said Pierce. "Moments away."

We plodded side by side through the deep snow. I wanted to run to the very top, but my body wouldn't let me.

When we finally rolled over the top of the mountain, my heart sank for a second. A slight slope of snow, about half the size of a football field, led to another high point.

Was this another fool's summit?

Pierce quickly put my mind at ease. "That mound up ahead. That is the summit, my dear friend."

On the gentle slope I began to speed up towards the very top of the mountain. I felt fantastic, both mentally and physically. Here at the top, moments from touching the six foot high cone of ice that marked the very summit, I was not only 'at' the top of the world, I 'felt' on top of the world!

I turned to see Pierce almost jogging to join me, grinning from ear to ear. He slowed a few paces from me, and then nodded, gesturing that it was all right for me to touch the frozen pointer that concluded this epic journey.

I reached out. And touched it.

A flood of unexpected and conflicting emotions poured over me. I was so happy to have made it to the top, and yet so sad that my time on the mountain was almost over. I felt proud to be standing there, yet humbled by the majesty of this living, breathing mountain that allowed me to walk upon its shoulders.

I'd done it.

I gave a sharp intake of breath and winked at Pierce, who stood erect with his hands on his hips, smiling like the father who just saw his son ride a bicycle for the first time.

"Pierce, thank you so much! It's been amazing. I'm happy to be up here, but sad at the same time that the journey is over."

"I know what you mean," he replied, glancing out over the orange and yellow carpet of sunlit clouds far below us. "Yet in many ways, your real journey has only just begun. Go home and love your family, and be kind and giving to all you encounter.

"Leave everyone you meet feeling better than they felt before bumping into you.

"Go back and create the life of your dreams, the happy, grateful and content life the Universe wants you to live. Really *live* that abundant life, and make every day a brilliant day full of love and joy.

"I have given you the tools to create any life you can imagine on the screen of your mind. All you have to do now is *do it!*"

I nodded in thanks and agreement. Pierce eased away from the summit and started to look back down the mountain at our footprints in the virgin snow.

"Can I have one more minute up here, Pierce?" I asked.

"Of course," he replied. "Feel free to watch the sun lower in the sky for a moment. Our descent back to the white temple will take no more than 30 minutes."

I looked out over the ocean of swirling orange mist and reflected on the process that had drawn me there.

The journey had actually started with the decision that I was going to stand on top of this mountain, when all around me said it could not be done.

From that seed of an idea, with the faith and determination to make it happen, to the cutting out of photos from brochures and adding images to my screensaver.

From the daily action in the direction of my dream, to the calculated risks taken in order to make this happen at all costs.

From keeping the faith that it would happen, even when at times it looked like it might not, to the final physically demanding challenge of actually trekking up the mountain.

Through all of these stages, like everything else I had ever achieved in my life, I had turned a thought from the eternal ether into a physical experience in the real world.

"Come," said Pierce. "It is time."

Through teary eyes I took one final look at the 360 degree splendour around me, the highest I had ever been on planet earth, physically, mentally, and spiritually.

I took a slow, deliberate intake of breath through my nostrils, and exhaled a much slower, audible out breath. I turned somewhat reluctantly on my heels, and joined Pierce to begin our trek from the top of the mountain.

*"So powerful is the light of unity that it
can illuminate the whole earth."*

— BAHÁ'U'LLÁH *(1817 – 1892), FOUNDER OF BÁBISM*

Unity

Since I returned from the mountain three years ago, my life has transformed completely.

I often think of the seven pillars that I saw in the white temple, and I've discovered that most people seem to have one or two very strong pillars that never weaken, and one or two that are neglected and therefore weak.

My own obvious weakness was in the financial pillar.

I used to attract to me just enough to do the basic things I had to do, and little else. That would have been fine if my list of things to do was rich, varied, and abundant, but it was not.

I held limiting beliefs around money, learned as a child from my parents. They loved me dearly, of that I have no doubt, and tried to do the very best for me. However, unknowingly, they imparted to me ideas like 'Money doesn't grow on trees' or 'What? Do you think I'm *made* of money!?'

While instilling a good work ethic, they also programmed my subconscious mind with the idea that you had to work very hard to make any 'real' money. As the child became an adult, I picked up the other limiting beliefs of family, friends, the media, and the general mass negative vibe of the area I was living in.

Consciously I was aware that I was different. I was aware that the regular 'work nine to five, retire at 65 with a gold watch' lifestyle was not for me. I didn't want to work in a factory, or an office. I wanted to be free.

So, in hindsight, I was very fortunate to have intuitively used many of the methods that Pierce shared with me on the mountain. That's how I ended up moving from my hometown, getting into performing, becoming a stuntman, breaking world records.

What I hadn't done until the trek up the sacred mountain, was use my God-given ability to create the perfect life 'on purpose'. That all changed on my return. The fact that you now hold this book in your hands, is a testament to that.

I'm slowly transforming my life in ways that make me want to leap out of bed in the morning to seize the day, to enjoy the journey through the highs and the lows, and to retire each evening with a clear vision of what I'm going to achieve the next day.

I've followed Pierce's advice to the letter, and my life has transformed and continues to do so.

My Own Seven Pillars

Physically I am in great shape, easily walking four or five miles a day before breakfast, able to comfortably jog for ten miles, and enjoying yoga daily since my return. I have been inspired to watch more carefully what I eat these days, currently enjoying a meat-free diet and doing a lot of cooking with fresh organic ingredients.

Mentally, I am much stronger now. I have an insatiable appetite for good books, and am expanding my mind every day. I'm presently studying for a coaching diploma and also practising Neuro Linguistic Programming.

I watch much less television, and if I do watch TV it's to watch something uplifting, or to learn from a documentary channel.

Financially I have gone through stops and starts since my return; it was a challenge to replace 39 years of 'lack' programming with a new 'abundance' program. In the first year of getting back, I managed to turn my best-ever annual income into a monthly income. All I did was follow the principles laid down in this book. I made the decision to do so, followed my intuition, and then took massive action to make it happen. Looking forward, I see my annual income reaching heights that, prior to my trek up the mountain, I would have found impossible to even imagine. Anything is possible!

Strangely enough, the more money that flows to me, it becomes less about the money and more about the good I can do with it. My whole future game plan is now about helping others to have what I have. The fact that I make money doing so is a simple bonus, and I see that as a means to more effectively help even more people. This book is my first step towards helping a greater number of people, because it can be helping others all over the world, no matter which country I might be in. It might even be helping people while I sleep. Wonderful!

From a spiritual viewpoint, I am in a much better place than I have ever been. I have read many great and inspiring books, and for a short while after my return, I struggled to grasp concepts such as the omnipresence of a thinking, conscious Universe. Pierce spoke of the Universe with great reverence, as a living, breathing, loving, consciousness that seeks further creation and fuller expression. Since my return, I have become at one with this Great Universe. I don't go to church. I respect everyone else's religious viewpoint. But I know God, and He knows me. That feels great.

This allows me to live a life of gratitude, of genuine thankfulness, something I never really did before my ascent of the spiritual mountain.

I say 'Thanks' in my mind a hundred times a day, not only for those coincidences that arrive right on time, but for the simple pleasures I used to take for granted—the sun on my face and the cool breeze on a hot summer day; the warmth of a fire on a cold evening; the scent of fresh herbs in a garden, or the smell of damp pine in a forest; the relaxing sound of a babbling brook, or the roar of a mighty waterfall; the spicy meal that explodes my taste buds, or the sweet dessert that makes my eyes roll back in my head with delight.

For the most part, my relationships have grown much stronger and deeper since I started living the principles outlined in this book. I've said goodbye to one or two people who no longer resonated with me, and tried to do so slowly and respectfully, wishing them well on their journey.

I've had some amazing experiences with my family where I have really listened, perhaps for the first time, to their needs and desires. I've then been able to cater for those needs and desires in a selfless way, bringing us all infinitely closer together.

Finally, I've taken on board what Pierce taught me about the importance of charity—not just about giving to others, but the feeling and the energy behind that giving.

One aspect of giving, the giving of my time, has led me to a whole new career. Since my return from the expedition, I have been out meeting students preparing for their final exams in readiness to leave school, college or university. I have explained the farfetched goals I had in mind when I was their age. The students laugh, some mock and jeer, as I confide in them that my childhood journal was full of hopes and dreams of learning to parachute, of becoming a movie stuntman, of starring in a James Bond movie, and of breaking World Records. People laughed at me and poked fun at me throughout my childhood, saying these things would never happen. Then I run a video on the projector, showing me doing all of these things.

The room is silent and I have their attention.

It gives me a warm feeling to make a room full of people really *think*.

I am a very ordinary person, and yet I do the things that I set out to do. And I do them because I follow the principles laid out in this book. The talks and lectures I give remind the guests that they can have, be or do anything they set their minds to. It reminds them to stay away from the doubters and the negative people who will talk them down to their level, and instead to stand tall and pursue their dreams with vigour.

My charity work has led from inspiring children to motivating adults, and I'm now creating a whole new, brighter future, not only for myself, but for all the people I interact with.

I could never have even considered this, were it not for the wise words of Pierce.

The Walk Off

I owe a debt of gratitude to the man I met, quite by chance (if you still believe in such things) by the crumbling wall in the foothills of that sacred mountain.

I miss him greatly.

Perhaps one day I will write a book about our walk back down the mountain, which was as full of magical surprises as the ascent.

Until then, I'd like to thank you from the depths of my soul for reading this book.

I hope that by digesting the wisdom within you can turn your life into the fantastic creative joy you were born to experience.

I know you can do it.

And when everything in your life becomes fabulous, every pillar as strong as the next, I know you will pass on this knowledge to help those around you.

I did.

I also know your life will go from strength to strength. For the more good you provide for others, the more goodness you attract into your own life. It is a Law of the Universe, as real as the Law of Gravity.

Visit this book as often as your intuition dictates. Really understand the messages within it, and go forth to create your amazing life.

Should you ever need help beyond this book, please pay me a visit at *www.CurtisRivers.com* where you'll find ways to follow me via social media and interact with other readers on the same path that you find yourself on now.

It is up to you whether you accept the challenge and begin to walk forward on this new-found path.

You create your own Universe as you go along.

As Lao Tzu said at the very beginning of this book, "The journey of a thousand miles begins with one step."

What will yours be?

FINDHORN PRESS

Life-Changing Books

Consult our catalogue online
(with secure order facility) on
www.findhornpress.com

For information on the Findhorn Foundation:
www.findhorn.org